QUIET
REFORMERS

QUIET REFORMERS

The Legacy of Early Victoria's
Bishop Edward and Mary Cridge

IAN MACDONALD & BETTY O'KEEFE

RONSDALE PRESS

QUIET REFORMERS
Copyright © 2010 Ian Macdonald and Betty O'Keefe

RONSDALE PRESS
3350 West 21st Avenue
Vancouver, BC, Canada V6S 1G7
www.ronsdalepress.com

Typesetting: Julie Cochrane, in Granjon 11.5 pt on 16
Cover Design: Cyanotype
Editing: Naomi Pauls, Paper Trail Publishing, & Noah Moscovitch
Paper: Rolland STSO

Ronsdale Press wishes to thank the following for their support of its publishing program: the Canada Council for the Arts, the Government of Canada through the Canada Book Plan, the British Columbia Arts Council, and the Province of British Columbia through the Book Publishing Tax Credit program.

Library and Archives Canada Cataloguing in Publication

Macdonald, Ian, 1928–
    Quiet reformers: the legacy of early Victoria's Bishop Edward and Mary Cridge / Ian Macdonald & Betty O'Keefe.

Includes bibliographical references and index.
ISBN 978-1-55380-107-8

    1. Cridge, Edward, 1817–1913. 2. Cridge, Mary. 3. Reformed Episcopal Church — Bishops — Biography. 4. Bishops — British Columbia — Victoria — Biography. 5. Bishops' spouses — British Columbia — Victoria — Biography. 6. Social reformers — British Columbia — Victoria — Biography. 7. Church of Our Lord (Victoria, B.C.) — History. 8. Victoria (B.C.) — Biography. I. O'Keefe, Betty, 1930– II. Title.

BX6093.C75M23 2010   283.3092'271128   c2010-904857-1

Printed in Canada by Marquis Book Printing, Montreal

To those who came before

To the memory of nineteenth- and early-twentieth-
century colonists who travelled halfway around
the world, often under difficult and dangerous
conditions, to find a better place and a better
life for themselves and their children.

In particular this book is dedicated to the
memory of Arthur Hortin, who left Kenilworth,
England, in the 1880s to follow a young lady named Mary
Ann Bearcroft from Erdington, whose family was moving
to Canada. The Bearcrofts settled in Vancouver, and
Arthur married Mary Ann at St. Paul's Anglican Church
there in 1890. They had seven children and made
their home in the Fairview district.

This book is also dedicated to the memory of
Dr. Edward E. Harper, pianist and composer, whose wife
died in Southport, England, as the family was preparing
to sail to Canada. Dr. Harper sailed without her and
arrived in Ottawa in 1910 with three grand pianos, three
children and a nanny to care for them. After one cold
winter he moved on to Vancouver, where he and the
family settled in 1911. He often performed at organ
recitals in Vancouver and Victoria churches.

ACKNOWLEDGEMENTS

The authors would like to thank David and Janet Laundy for sharing the letters and diaries written by Edward and Mary Cridge and for their personal observations and comments during the writing of this book. Our thanks also go to Sylvia Van Kirk, archivist at the Church of Our Lord, and to Iris Franklin, genealogy librarian in Birmingham, England, for their assistance in checking details for us and answering some of the questions that arose during our research. We also thank Ronsdale Press, our publisher, for undertaking to print this story about two people who had a significant impact on the community and the way of life in early Victoria and on Vancouver Island.

CONTENTS

Introduction

In the twenty-first century, as instant communication, supersonic transport and ubiquitous technology dominate our lives, it becomes more and more difficult to imagine what life was like for the settlers who arrived on the Pacific coast in the 1840s and 1850s. There were no telephones, telegraph service was yet to arrive, and it took a year or more to receive an answer to a letter mailed to England from British Columbia.

During the first fifty years, it took all the courage, resolve, faith, hard work and adaptability of those who ventured to the Pacific coast to surmount their many disappointments and sorrows. Roads and rail lines were non-existent. There were no schools or hospitals. Sanitation was primitive and when disease struck it was with devastating results, killing many. Life expectancy was only fifty years.

Some of the new arrivals were filled with the spirit of adventure; others were fleeing grinding, unending poverty; a few fled from persecution; and the most dedicated came to provide religious guidance and schooling for the emerging community. The two principals of this story lived much longer than most of their contemporaries, and they had great influence on the moral fibre of the people who knew and admired them. Their experiences taxed these adventurous and deeply religious pioneers emotionally and physically, but they came west prepared to overcome adversities in search of a new, better life for themselves and their contemporaries.

Reverend (later Bishop) Edward and Mary Cridge played a key role in the social, religious and political development of the land that would become the province of British Columbia. When they arrived in 1855, there were only three hundred settlers in or near Victoria, with others spread out over Vancouver Island. The Native population was estimated to be around twenty-six thousand. On the mainland, the European population was scant and scattered and the city of Vancouver did not yet exist. The couple came to Fort Victoria, the Hudson's Bay Company's lonely bastion at the southern tip of Vancouver Island, where they helped to guide its progress from a company outpost to the capital of the westernmost province in a new nation.

Edward Cridge was hired as a chaplain and for a time was the only Protestant minister in the community. A man of great social conscience, he had a liberality in his views that some of his brethren did not share. He reached beyond sermons from the pulpit and worked constantly for the betterment of all. Mary Cridge, who shared his convictions, was the rock to which he clung for love and support throughout their long lives together.

They had been educated in the British style of the times, with its emphasis on strict Victorian principles, but their Church of England school background gave them the freedom of thought to practise a way of life built on democratic and progressive ideals. Their contributions to social reform included encouraging education for all, caring for orphans, working alongside Natives, helping to establish a hospital and discouraging racial discrimination, as well as teaching a simple evangelical religious message. Edward and Mary Cridge made a significant contribution to the development and history of British Columbia.

I

Edward and Mary

On a mild spring day, in the fields behind Christ Church, at West Ham, Essex, near London in the south of England, a young woman named Mary Winmill had just returned from a long walk with a man who, in the past three years, had become her close friend and confidant. She waved goodbye to him at the garden gate and walked slowly down the pathway, admiring the flowers. As she entered the house, she shook her head before her mother could ask the question so frequently voiced of late. No, Edward had not suggested marriage, and Mary, as well as her mother, wondered whether he ever would.

Mary Winmill was no longer a young girl, but an intelligent, attractive dark-haired woman, aged twenty-seven, and she was extremely fond of the young curate who seemed to enjoy her company so much. The two often discussed Sunday sermons and the teaching of young children. Their lives were centred on the activities at Christ Church, where Mary was a schoolteacher and Edward was the newly ordained curate. She had hoped that on this particularly glorious day he would propose marriage, but he remained hesitant, and she knew he felt marriage might interfere with his work as a minister. There were, however, events taking place half a world away that would change the prospects for the Reverend Edward Cridge and Mary Winmill, making it possible for them to begin the great adventure that lay ahead.

Edward Cridge was born on December 17, 1817, in the small village of Bratton-Flemming, Devonshire, in southwest England, the son of John and Grace Dyer Cridge. His mother died when he was a small boy; his father, a deeply religious schoolmaster, tutored his son at home in the early years, a major factor in his early educational development and achievements. John Cridge's hopes for his son were realized when at the age of nineteen the boy became the third master of the grammar school at Oundle in Northamptonshire. Although he was young for this relatively senior position, Edward was well received by the headmaster, who valued him as "competent to undertake mathematics...Latin authors...and junior forms of Greek." He deemed Edward to be "active, efficient and trustworthy."[1]

After Edward Cridge had taught for six years, the religious beliefs fostered by his father led him to further study with a view to becoming a clergyman. He attended St. Peter's College, Cambridge, and in 1848 passed examinations in theology and graduated with an honours degree in mathematics on February 6. It had been a heavy load involving many long hours of study, but he enjoyed academia. Cridge was a thoughtful, serious man but did not exclude himself from other aspects of life. He had a short, stocky figure and was a good athlete and horseman, having jumped as many as seventeen five-barred gates one after the other. He also developed a lifelong love of music, and in time became an accomplished cellist. Cridge was a founding member of the Cambridge Musical Society, a group he supported throughout his life and which exists to this day. During difficult times in his life, music gave him much comfort.

After graduating from Cambridge, Cridge was ordained a deacon at Norwich Cathedral, and appointed assistant curate and second master in the grammar school at Walsham, Norfolk. On February 24, 1850, he was made a full priest of the church at a ceremony conducted by Bishop Samuel Hinds. Several months later, he was appointed a vicar at Christ Church in the Marsh District on the Romford Road, the newest and poorest church in the parish of West Ham, a village near London. It was here that he met Mary Winmill.

One of his early parishioners described the Reverend Cridge as a man with a large head but an impressive profile. In later years he was heavily bearded. He seldom smiled during a church service, but his face was described as serene, with a pleasant, sincere expression that could not be ignored, for it emphasized that he *believed* the words he spoke in his gentle, refined voice. He was never a passionate preacher, but particularly in his later years he was a powerful figure in the pulpit and in society. His success with his parishioners centred on his quiet-spoken, deep-seated convictions, his belief in God, and the principles by which he lived.

Edward Cridge was as unquestioning in his desire to follow the teachings of the Church of England as he was in his loyalty to his country, his Queen and her empire. He firmly believed, however, that sweeping social reforms were needed and that the Church must play a leading role in effecting them. His commitment to the betterment of humanity had been established in his early years by his father and in lessons preached to him from the pulpit. He demonstrated his compassion at Cambridge, where he participated in raising funds for the thousands of people who were dying in Ireland because of famine caused by the potato blight, a catastrophe that too few others at the time found to be of much concern.

Cridge was brought up in Victorian England, with its worldwide empire on which the sun never set. For some time there had been a growing need for clergymen to minister to the men and women from Britain who were leaving their home shores for foreign lands. The Church of England saw its horizons broadening and undertook to spread the gospel to the inhabitants of these far-flung lands. Cridge could have looked to a future in a large, well-established church in England, in the land he loved and knew so well. Instead he took an unanticipated opportunity to make a dramatic change in his life — to leave England. But he had important reasons for the decision, which he soon shared with Mary Winmill.

A growing schism had developed within the Church, a philosophical argument between those who preferred the High Church ritualistic type of service, reminiscent of the Roman Catholic Church, and those who favoured the simpler Low Church, or evangelical, form of worship. Cridge believed that the Church must follow the path set out by the Protestant reformers, and he rejected the exaggerated emphasis on ritualism in the High Church, feeling it was too close to Roman Catholicism. In West Ham, an established conservative parish, some members of the congregation believed Cridge was preaching Calvinism and predetermination, rather than the established Church doctrine with which they were familiar. They resented Cridge's approach and complained to the dean, his superior at West Ham.

The dean himself favoured High Church ritual, and in order to ease the tension in the parish, he suggested that Cridge take a leave of absence or look for another, more suitable parish. While Cridge had many redeeming qualities, he was also stubborn, and although he seldom showed it openly, he was easily riled by criticism. He refused to move to a church where the congregation would accept his Low Church beliefs. Fortunately the dean, a man of many years' experience, found a way to resolve the issue. He learned in August 1854 that the Hudson's Bay Company was looking for a new chaplain for its fort on Vancouver Island, where a new settlement was being established. He suggested that Edward Cridge apply.

Like so many others in Great Britain during the previous two centuries, Cridge jumped at the chance to join the "Company of Adventurers." He knew little of Vancouver Island, only that it was a largely undeveloped territory with a sparse population. He had corresponded with a fellow minister he had met at Cambridge, the Reverend Robert John Staines, who had previously held the position of chaplain at the fort, after arriving there in 1849. Staines had been hired by the chief factor of Fort Victoria, James Douglas, and had travelled with his wife to the far-off fur-trading post, which had been given the authority by the Crown to tap the area's abundant resources.

In his reports and letters to England, Staines described the sweeping forests of mighty trees, waters teeming with fish and the bounty of fur-bearing animals. There were minerals to be sought and there was land to be cultivated, but the colony lacked people to do it all. Although Staines had written about the territory in glowing terms, he complained about the authoritarian role played by James Douglas, who, he said, was a difficult man. Staines' comments about Douglas did not deter Cridge from considering the job. Not only did Cridge realize that he was in a crisis situation with his own church, but he felt that the position offered an opportunity to teach the principles of Christianity in an area where they were largely unknown. He also believed the offer was "God sent," and therefore one which he could not ignore. As company chaplain, he would act as regional minister for the Hudson's Bay Company and provide Christian teaching for the children in the community.

Writing in his diary at a later date, Cridge explained he had no misgivings about deciding to leave England, believing that "the great clearness with which our heavenly father marked our path from the beginning" made every step so plain "that there was no mistaking it."[2] His religious views also seemed suited to a frontier life and the breaking of new ground. Years later he stated simply, "Intercourse with the world is not forbidden, only conformity of the world. Religion is of the will and not of compulsion." His beliefs are explained in a bible studies book that he wrote: "It follows that it is the will of God that nations should enjoy the inestimable benefits of freedom." Cridge contended that "the will of God and a sound governing system on earth assured the progress of freedom and created a balancing power which tends to preserve it from anarchy and wildness."[3]

* * *

Apart from his two sisters, Mary and Elizabeth, Mary Winmill was the only woman with whom Edward Cridge felt totally at ease, the only one he knew well enough to confide in, and when he finally admitted it, the woman he had grown to love. Until her father died in 1853, Mary Winmill lived in a spacious home in Romford, Essex, where she spent much of her time with her family. Born at Dagenham, Essex, on April 15, 1827, she had not travelled far. She had one younger unmarried sister. Like many women of her era, the Church was the centre of her social and family life. She had been educated in a church school. After her father's death and the loss of his income, she had taken a job teaching at the school in Christ Church. She was a striking woman with black hair and blue eyes, which often held a suggestion of a twinkle despite her demure Victorian upbringing. She was described by her mother's friends as a pleasant, thoughtful, pretty young woman, but at twenty-seven most felt she should marry soon or face spinsterhood.

Through her participation in church activities and her teaching, Mary had come to know Edward Cridge, and they had become close friends. They took long walks on the moor, discussing many things, a topic for a sermon Edward was planning or a problem that had come up at church or in the school. In Edward's daily diary he often referred to discussions with Mary, but did not at first express any special feelings. He was a serious man, and his diary was a record of his daily routine rather than his hopes, plans or ambitions. Following his graduation from Cambridge, he had initially avoided thoughts of marriage because he felt that such a commitment would be a hindrance in his pursuit of God's work.

At almost thirty-seven, he finally admitted his feelings for Mary in one of the few personal comments in his diary: "There was one subject that occupied a large share of my thoughts. I had long struggled against it, but in vain; and that was my love for Mary Winmill. If love and reason alike lead me to decide whenever God should place me in suitable circumstances, I would ask Mary Winmill to share with me the journey of life in work of the gospel."

Those "suitable circumstances" appeared quite suddenly after Edward applied for the Hudson's Bay Company post in Fort Victoria. His application stated that he would strive to do the work of the Heavenly Father and promote the best interests of the colony. The colonial office and the Company pondered his application and finally offered a five-year contract with the option of a renewal, plus free passage for himself and his party to the fort and for their return to England, if so desired at the end of the agreement. He was urged to marry before leaving because there were few, if any, eligible women in the small community around the fort, and a wife could help him greatly. He knew immediately that he wanted Mary to go with him.

After receiving the offer from the colonial office in London, Edward hurried to find Mary. He met her as she was leaving her home to attend evening services at Christ Church. They walked together for a while instead of carrying on to the church, and Edward asked Mary to marry him. She agreed.

As part of his proposal, Edward outlined the hazards of the ocean voyage that would serve as their honeymoon and take them to an alien, wild land. He kept nothing from his future bride, reiterating all the information he had received about Fort Victoria and admitting that he knew little of the near wilderness that would be their home. He told her that there had been problems finding suitable ministers for the West Coast and that his predecessor, the Reverend Staines, had found the governor difficult. Staines had been heading home to England with a petition to oust the governor when his boat sank off Cape Flattery, taking him to his grave.

Edward explained it all as best he could, acknowledging that even after a successful voyage they would face many uncertainties and a lifestyle far removed from anything either of them had known. His stipend from the colonial office was three hundred pounds per year to act as district minister, and he would receive another hundred per year to provide services as chaplain to the Hudson's Bay Company. They would be provided with a parsonage and a hundred acres of land for cultivation. Until the land was

Edward Cridge (BC ARCHIVES, G-02055)

productive — and they would require help to accomplish this — they would receive sufficient rations to provide for themselves and any others who accompanied them.

Thrilled rather than daunted by the prospect of her new life with Edward, Mary accepted the challenge. She put her faith in God and the man she loved. Cridge wrote in his diary when he returned home: "We walked across the marshes and she yielded her consent to my suit." His simple words failed to reflect the joy and excitement he must have felt about their engagement.

Although Mary was delighted with the proposal, her mother was distraught at the prospect of her daughter's impending departure. Marrying the minister was acceptable, but leaving the country where she was born

Mary Cridge (BC ARCHIVES, A-01304)

for a new, dangerous life in an unknown wilderness so far away was a frightening prospect. But Mrs. George Winmill understood that after her husband's recent death, the family had few financial resources and, without this marriage, Mary faced an uncertain future. The overriding factor, in the end, was Mary's happiness. Before long Mrs. Winmill consented to her daughter's wishes and gave her blessing to the union.

As time was short, Edward and Mary were quickly married on September 14, 1854, in a simple ceremony performed by a close friend, the Reverend F. W. Davis, at All Saints Church. There was no elaborate dress for either of them: Edward wore his clerical collar, and Mary, a high-necked bodice and brimmed bonnet. The couple received a silver chalice and a purse of money as a wedding present from the congregation, along with many good wishes.[4] Mary's excited pupils scattered flowers on the path before the open carriage as the newlyweds departed. Their marriage was a partnership that lasted more than fifty years, marked often with outstanding achievements but also fraught at times with danger, deprivation and adjustments to great change.

The new job solved many problems for Edward, both in his relations with the parish and in his personal situation. His elderly, ailing father had badly mismanaged his financial affairs and was facing debtor's prison. As soon as Edward's application was accepted, he arranged for fifty pounds to be paid annually into a bank in Devon for his father's care. Edward's two unmarried sisters, Elizabeth and Mary, agreed to see their father settled and then follow their brother to help teach children at Fort Victoria. With his father's sickness and his older brother Richard's recent death, Edward felt responsible for his sisters' well-being. He could also use their skills as teachers in his new position.

After some discussion with Mary's mother, it was decided that in addition to Edward's two sisters at least three more people would be required to help out in Fort Victoria. They were to be Mr. and Mrs. John Raby and Mary Herbert, the family's three servants. With the death of her husband and her daughter's departure, Mrs. Winmill planned to move to a smaller cottage. The three servants were offered assistance in finding new employment in England or the chance to follow the Cridges to Victoria. They chose the latter. It would be a rugged life, but it was also an exciting opportunity to start afresh, to help develop a new community and to aid the newly married Mary Cridge, to whom they were attached. It is doubtful that Edward and Mary could have fulfilled their duties so well without their assistance.

Their days in England now numbered, the five organized the packing of their belongings and said their farewells to family and friends. Although they were leaving homes where they had lived for many years, excitement about their life ahead quelled most of their misgivings. Edward and Mary drove off in high spirits for the Port of Gravesend, delighted with their marriage and the prospect of their life together.

2

Sailing Southern Seas

I t was to be a long honeymoon for the newlyweds. On a sunny September 20, 1854, six days after their nuptials, Edward and Mary Cridge watched the shoreline of their homeland disappear as the sails of the *Marquis of Bute* caught the wind and the ship set a course from Gravesend southwest across the Atlantic, bound for Cape Horn and the far Pacific Ocean. Edward's sisters, Elizabeth and Mary, remained in England to settle their father before making the journey to join their brother and his bride. Beside the couple at the ship's rail stood the three family retainers from the Winmill home. As the small group watched their beloved England fade from view, each of them must have wondered whether they would ever see it again.

The *Marquis of Bute* was a three-masted, 562-ton barque built in Quebec City in 1840. She was named after an aristocrat who had extensive land holdings, including an ancestral home on the Isle of Bute, located in the River Clyde in Scotland. Originally the ship had plied the Atlantic between Quebec and Wales before it was assigned to longer voyages. On this occasion, the *Marquis* had been chartered by the Hudson's Bay Company to transport people and cargo around Cape Horn to the new fort on Vancouver Island. The ship was as well fitted for passengers as any other sailing ship of the era, but accommodations were spartan. On board were twenty-three passengers in all: seven in cabin class (including the newlyweds) and sixteen in steerage. Reading the few available books, playing card games, conversing with other travellers and walking the deck were the only diversions during the long voyage. Around them churned the endless sea, and inevitably the first week was the worst for the passengers. Edward wrote tersely in his diary, "We were most of us very ill with seasickness." It was a problem that would plague him for much of the voyage and often force him to take to his bunk.

Mary was less afflicted with seasickness and quickly became accustomed to the ship's constant motion. She was fascinated by the sea and untroubled by the hazards of ship travel, although she had been told that strange illnesses often swept through ships, and starvation was an ever-present threat when voyages were delayed. She also heard stories from other passengers that upon occasion the silence surrounding a becalmed vessel could drive some poor souls to madness. Mary was content to put her trust in God, her new husband and the faith she had learned since childhood. Boredom rarely plagued her, for she was an observant woman with an interest in learning all she could from the journey. She marvelled at the intricate rigging above the vessel and the sails that caught the wind and powered the *Marquis*. The wonders of the ocean entranced her, as did the brilliant, starry skies of the southern hemisphere.

Mary passed some of the time by writing about her experiences. She kept an extensive diary and wrote letters to her mother and sister and her husband's two sisters about the sights she witnessed on the voyage. She wrote most often to Elizabeth, Edward's younger sister, a woman she had never met but had felt a kinship with since she had learned that they had been baptized on the same day. Part of each day Mary spent in the cramped cabin with her ailing husband, telling him what she had seen. Seated at the tiny desk built against the wall, she wrote her letters home, unconcerned by the dim light of the cabin or the groaning of the timbers as the ship ploughed its way ever southward.

Mary was grateful to Captain John Moir of the *Marquis of Bute*, whom she found to be a kindly man. He took the time to give her lessons in basic astronomy as they stood on deck looking up into the skies. He pointed out the Southern Cross and other constellations; she was awed by the millions of stars spread across the wide heavens above her.

There were also hundreds of birds, some she had never seen before. She saw an albatross with a nine-foot wing span, and cape pigeons, which she thought were the most beautiful of all the birds. Writing to her sister-in-law, she described these pigeons as "black and white with darkly tinted head plumage gradually softening in colour, affording a sweet contrast to the snowy plumage of their breasts."[1]

One day the sighting of whales in the lonely seas created great excitement among the passengers. Mary was amazed at their size: "as large as a boat." She was fascinated too by the strange luminous things she saw moving in the ocean, and when a ship's officer dipped a basket in the sea and brought one aboard she described it as "a curious thing, half animal, half vegetable, so it seems. The colour was dull gray when either in water or out but when we touched it, it was luminous, the colour a bright pea green."

These were the highlights Mary Cridge described to her relatives as the pleasures that overcame a "troublesome voyage," for the days could be boiling hot or freezing cold, and the seas were often white-capped and stormy. Moreover, when fresh supplies loaded in England ran out, those aboard ate monotonous, tasteless rations, often badly prepared. Passengers faced a constant dampness and an almost total lack of amenities. The longer the ship was out of touch with the rest of the world, the more pervasive became an eerie feeling of forlorn detachment, a sense of abandonment that became magnified whenever they encountered fog.

The Reverend Cridge conducted morning prayers and evening services aboard the ship on the open deck — whenever weather permitted. But Mary worried about his condition, as he continued to suffer from seasickness. Eventually, she noted: "His daily evening service is discontinued with the exception of Wednesday evenings. I think the dear fellow would scarcely have given it up had it not been for my persuasion that it was really a duty to rest now so that he may be strengthening (if God will) for the many important duties that await him in the new land."

Despite Edward's condition, the voyage was relatively free of serious illness. In the days of sail, wooden ships were breeding grounds for a variety of diseases, including tuberculosis and typhoid, and many would-be pioneers did not live to set foot on a foreign shore. Burials at sea were common, with babies and young children the most vulnerable. Seldom was there a doctor aboard, unless he was travelling as a passenger. Women with rudimentary knowledge of care and nursing helped their families and others as best they could when sickness struck.

One day as the vessel fought its way westward through giant green roiling waves, Mary Cridge stared into the distance at a spectacle that held her spellbound. It was a huge iceberg, something she had never dreamed she would view on the open sea. She dashed below deck to tell Edward. Bundling him up in a blanket, she helped him to the main deck, where they stood together, gazing in awe at the icy jewel floating before them.

Despite spending months at sea and her husband's frequent illness, Mary Cridge was very much a woman in love. The voyage was an exciting adventure, different from anything she had imagined. She only wished Edward were in better health. She confided her feelings to her sister-in-law: "You may feel quite sure, dear Elizabeth, that the personal intimacy and companionship of husband and wife, have made me value him even more deeply. I need not say to you because you know him, but of myself I may say that I feel unworthy of such a companion and such a treasure. Yet I daily pray that God may teach me what I must know and fit me to perform all the duties which devolve upon me."

Separation from her family in England touched Mary deeply on Christmas Day. She missed her mother and sister from whom she had never before been apart. She knew how different their Christmas would be without her, and how painfully they would miss her. She wrote that almost all of the passengers and crew attended the Christmas morning service conducted by her husband. That day they also enjoyed a pleasant surprise, the result of careful planning by Captain Moir, who produced an amazingly varied Christmas menu for all aboard, a contrast to the monotony of their usual fare. The steerage passengers had meat and plum pudding while those in cabin class had fowl, ham, plum pudding and mince pies. "The pudding was nice and larger than I have ever seen one before," Mary added.

After many days at sea, two passengers sought solace from the boredom of the voyage in ways that, though far from surprising, created a stir aboard the ship. Among the steerage passengers returning to the colony was a man named Chapman, a servant of Captain William Mouat, who was a Hudson's Bay Company employee. Also aboard was a woman named Mrs. Brown, en route to the colony to join her husband. As Edward Cridge wrote in his diary, "An intimacy has sprung up of a nature to cause much scandal in the ship." Captain Moir announced that because of this affair steerage passengers were barred from the quarterdeck, presumably a corner of which had been the place of the couple's tryst. Steerage passengers complained en masse and the ban was soon reversed, although the impenitent Chapman and Mrs. Brown remained excluded. What eventually happened to the lovers when they reached Vancouver Island is lost to history.

The stout little ship bucked heavy seas and winds as it struggled to round Cape Horn, the only route to the Pacific, and the *Marquis* made no headway for several days. Mary realized it could have been worse when the ship's boatswain told her of a trip that had been halted by the elements for several weeks. When those on the *Marquis* finally glimpsed land, and the passengers realized they were looking at the southern tip of South America, there was great excitement for all aboard. The shoreline, the first Mary had seen after three months at sea, reminded her of the last verse of one of her favourite hymns. She repeated it with her husband as they walked the decks and studied the stark, desolate mountains of Tierra del Fuego:

> And when we regain the land,
> How happy shall we be,
> How shall we bless this Mighty Hand,
> That leads us through the sea.

Mary described with pleasure the dramatic sight of the lonely islands they passed, and their tall, snow-capped mountains: "The sight of two islands filled us with longing . . . one is about sixty miles in length and composed of high barren mountains covered with snow, it is uninhabited. On the other are the lofty mountains of Tierra del Fuego. . . . we found it difficult to leave the deck." Both husband and wife yearned for the end of their voyage but knew that months still lay ahead before they would finish their trip up the west coast of America to reach their final destination and set foot for good on solid soil.

About one feature of the voyage, however, Mary Cridge felt they were most fortunate, and this was the time of year they were travelling: "As the time of our being at the Cape was summer season, not four of the twenty-four hours of each day were dark, in consequence the inconvenience of darkness was far less than had it been in winter. As it was we frequently felt cold notwithstanding many wraps. There are no stoves on board and we saw rough weather, such as we had never witnessed before." She recounted stoically, "Yet many comforts and blessings were mingled with little trials by our blessed Father, and when you are called to take so long a voyage, may He deal with you dear sister as gently as He has dealt with us."

Some of Mary's letters to her mother and other relatives were carried back to England by ships encountered in the region of Cape Horn. Mary explained that this was not an easy transfer: a small boat lowered from the *Marquis* had to be rowed through heavy seas and the delivery made as quickly as possible while the ships jockeyed to stay close to each other.

The *Marquis* finally found favourable winds and cleared the Horn on

December 30. The captain set a course northwest into the Pacific en route for the Sandwich (Hawaiian) Islands. The Hudson's Bay Company had a fort on these islands, at this time a British protectorate. The seas became calmer and the weather warmer as they headed north. Finally, after some five months at sea, in February 1855, land was once again sighted. The call came first from the crow's nest — "Land ho!" — and then from the decks. Cabins quickly emptied as the crew and passengers crowded the rails and watched the mountains of Oahu grow larger as the ship approached Honolulu's harbour. Everyone was eager to disembark as soon as possible to escape the constant motion of the sea. Mary was pleased when a woman disembarking at Oahu said she had been much impressed by the Reverend Cridge's sermons and bible teaching. Later Mary wrote that the woman had "considerably benefited" from Edward's explanations.

As they walked along the shore arm-in-arm, Edward and Mary feasted their eyes on the magnificent flowers and foliage, and inhaled the rich fragrance that filled the air, a marked change from the smell of the sea. At Honolulu, the Cridges stayed at a private home for about three weeks. It began as a wonderful vacation in the sun, the two of them daily walking the long sand beaches, but then Mary was unexpectedly stricken with an illness peculiar to the area. "I was preparing letters for home when I felt a pain in my stomach, aches in my limbs and cold shivers. Accordingly I laid myself down and very soon the symptoms changed to burning fever and violent headache."

A doctor was sent for who diagnosed and treated her fever. Mary noted, "He sent me two doses which with God's blessing were the means of relieving my pain. Although until nine o'clock that same day I felt worse than I had been, yet afterwards I became so rapidly better as to be able next day to go to the dining room." Edward was given the same medicine in the hopes that he would avoid the illness. Mary described the disease as painful and tedious, but also said no one seemed to die of it: "The inhabitants of Honolulu seem to look upon it as we should in England, a bilious attack or some such trifle, yet they are careful to attend to it immediately."

Just before the couple's departure from the islands, Edward received a letter from his sister Elizabeth stating that their father had died. She and her sister Mary were preparing for his funeral and the sale of their few belongings. They would depart for Fort Victoria in three or four months, as soon as a ship became available. That day Edward and Mary held a small service of their own in honour of the man who had taught Edward so much. And then the *Marquis* set sail for Vancouver Island, where they would step ashore to live behind the palisades and sentries of a rudimentary fort on the western edge of North America.

3

Fort Victoria in Mid-Century

The sighting of a ship heading towards their tranquil harbour at the end of March 1855 created welcome excitement in the small Vancouver Island settlement of Fort Victoria. As the *Marquis of Bute* drew near and its flags were identified, residents saw that the ship was from England. It would be bringing newcomers and a cargo of mail, newspapers, books, clothing, badly needed general supplies and much-desired personal items, ordered in some cases more than a year earlier. When the weather-beaten vessel dropped anchor at Ross Bay, off Clover Point, people gathered on shore to see if they could identify friends or relatives aboard. Because of the lateness of the hour and the ebbing tide, the ship would not be able to navigate the rocky entrance into the quiet inner harbour by the fort until the next day. Then Edward and Mary would meet for the first time the man who ruled the colony and who would greatly influence their future.

James Douglas (NANAIMO DISTRICT MUSEUM, I1-152)

In the middle of the nineteenth century, James Douglas, chief factor on Vancouver Island for the Hudson's Bay Company, was conducting Company affairs and establishing new settlements along the Pacific coast. He was a highly motivated, disciplined, stern and sometimes benevolent despot. If Edward and Mary Cridge were not to run into the same problems that the Reverend Staines had encountered at Fort Victoria, they had to learn quickly, not only the history and social challenges of the outpost they were joining, but also the background and temperament of the man in charge.

Douglas was an atypical leader for the period, often referred to irreverently as the "Scotch West Indian." He was born in Demerara, British Guyana, on August 15, 1803, a son of the Scottish merchant John Douglas and a free Creole from Barbados, Margaret Ann Tefler. He was sent to Scotland for his education when he was twelve years old. At sixteen, he was apprenticed to the Montreal-based North West Company, a rival in the North American fur trade to the Hudson's Bay Company. The two companies merged in 1821, when the British parliament expanded the Hudson's Bay Company trading area under licence to encompass all of Rupert's Land. The Company then controlled more than one-third of what is now Canada.

The assertive, no-nonsense George Simpson, governor of Rupert's Land, described Douglas when they first met as "a stout, powerful active man of good conduct and respectable abilities," who could become "furiously violent when aroused."[1] Simpson was impressed by Douglas's abilities and directed his rise up through the ranks of the expanded Company.

In 1828, at Fort St. James, in the rugged central part of what was later to become the province of British Columbia, Douglas met and shortly thereafter married Amelia, the part-Native daughter of Chief Factor William Connolly. As a result of his own mixed racial background as well as Amelia's, Douglas was a proponent of racial equality, and tried to establish a tradition of acceptance and tolerance.

Douglas's career on the coast began in 1830 when Simpson sent him to Fort Vancouver, at the mouth of the Columbia River. Douglas became chief trader there in 1835 and chief factor four years later. As his career progressed and his power increased, Douglas became increasingly autocratic and egotistical, his self-image bolstered by his achievements and rapid advancement. Despite these shortcomings, he remained conscientious and was always concerned for the colonists who worked with him or settled in his territory.[2]

By the early 1840s, the trading company and the British government could see clearly that the United States intended to expand its territorial ambitions and holdings north from San Francisco as far as possible. The Hudson's Bay Company headquarters in the West had been at Fort Vancouver on the Columbia River, but the Company also maintained posts at Fort Langley, on the Fraser River, and farther north at Fort Simpson (near Prince Rupert). Because of increasing U.S. settlement on the Oregon coast and America's efforts to move its influence north, the Hudson's Bay Company decided to abandon Fort Vancouver, to bolster Fort Langley, and to seek another port to replace Fort Vancouver.

In 1842, thirteen years before the Cridges arrived, Douglas set out from Fort Langley with six men in the *Cadboro* to explore possible locations, and settled on Victoria. Initially, relatively few colonists arrived to settle the area. The slow growth was not a concern for the Company, which saw itself as a trader of goods, but England wanted immigrants to occupy the land and so establish a larger British presence in the hopes of staving off further U.S. expansion northward. But settlers were held back by the uncertainty over who would have final jurisdiction. Even by the time the Cridges arrived in 1855, there was still some doubt as to whether the Americans might make a play for Vancouver Island. In fact, the Reverend Cridge had been brought in part to deepen the sense that Victoria was a genuine colony and so attract more settlers. Deeply embroiled in the debate over the border with the United States, England ordered Royal Navy warships to step up their presence and increase patrols. The navy established a base very close to Victoria at Esquimalt, and Douglas welcomed each new ship personally as it arrived at the base.

The increasing number of Americans moving north into the Columbia River Basin ultimately dashed any lingering British hopes of retaining the territory, and in 1846, the United States and Great Britain finally signed an agreement extending the forty-ninth parallel as the international boundary through the area. The agreement, known as the Oregon Treaty, helped reduce international tension but did not eliminate it entirely. England retained Vancouver Island in the treaty and James Douglas was appointed the Company agent for the area.

As the Cridges were to learn, the growth of Fort Victoria had been painfully slow. Douglas arrived at the site, near where the Victoria legislative buildings now stand, on March 14, 1843, aboard the *Beaver*, a tiny ship that was the first steam-driven craft on the Pacific coast. With a team of about twenty men, each earning a princely seventeen pounds a year, and accompanied by a pioneer Roman Catholic missionary, Father J. B. Z. Bolduc, Douglas ordered the clearing of a flat area on a small bluff above a protected harbour on the southern tip of Vancouver Island. He chose the site for the fort carefully. He was not usually sentimental but fondly wrote after first viewing the area, "This place itself appears a perfect 'Eden' in the midst of the dreary wilderness of the North West coast and so different in its general aspect, from the wooded rugged regions around, that one might be pardoned for supposing it had dropped from the clouds into its present position."[3]

Responsibility for building the fort was assigned to Charles Ross and completed by Roderick Finlayson, the son of an Irish immigrant sheep farmer. Finlayson directed men equipped with only axes, saws and chisels to build a palisade that was about one hundred yards square. The Natives were intrigued by Finlayson's project and came to watch. They were soon recruited to provide the twenty-two-foot-long cedar trees being used to

Bastion at Fort Victoria, c. 1850 (BC ARCHIVES, A-00903 / PHOTO: MAYNARD)

construct the walls of the stockade. They were loaned axes to fell the trees, and the negotiated price for their labour was one blanket for every forty logs supplied. The original corner bastion at the fort was three storeys high and when completed was mounted with blunderbusses and muskets. As Mary Cridge was later to observe, the guns did not look as though they would be effective against any genuine invading force.

The days were long, the work was hard, but the summer weather was fair and by October two large dwellings and a sizable storehouse had been completed. One of these was where the Cridges would be lodged when they first arrived. Work had also begun on a meeting hall. The *Beaver* was pushed into service to bring horses and cattle to the new location, and some of the men began to make rudimentary plows from oak branches and the iron hoops removed from barrels. In December 1843, five acres of wheat were planted, the first crop for the new fort. The food supply was augmented by salmon and other seafood plentiful in surrounding waters.

At one point the new bastion was to be called Princess Adelaide, and then for a time it was known as Fort Albert, after Queen Victoria's consort, but on June 10, 1843, the Council of the Northern Department of the Hudson's Bay Company, meeting at Fort Garry in the east, resolved that the new western headquarters would be named Fort Victoria in honour of the young Queen of England.

The settlement's importance as a vital trading post was established with the export of logs to San Francisco almost as soon as the main rooms in the palisade were complete. Three years later a sawmill was constructed near the fort to provide lumber for new building. By 1853, only ten years after its birth, some planning for the environs of Fort Victoria had been completed. The surveyors J. D. Pemberton and B. W. Pearse had mapped out a townsite, and soon small shops and saloons began to appear and the rough paths gradually became trodden into hard-packed roads. Pemberton had included a hundred-acre site for the Church of England, where the church, parsonage, school and adjacent agricultural land would be located. In 1855, however, the year the Cridges arrived, the town was only beginning to emerge.

4

The Early Years

On April 1, 1855, Edward and Mary Cridge disembarked on Vancouver Island. On the morning of their arrival in Victoria harbour, Governor James Douglas strode through the crowd to meet the dory he had sent to bring them ashore. The Cridges were helped over the gunwale by one of the ship's sailors, after which Douglas warmly shook hands with them both. The new chaplain was a welcome sight for the governor, who had waited nearly a year for his arrival.

After months afloat and despite the dismal rainy day, Edward and Mary were more than pleased to set foot, if a little unsteadily, on the land that was to become their home. "Douglas' welcome was enthusiastic as he conducted us to the Fort," Edward wrote in his diary. "We received an invitation from His Excellency, Governor Douglas, to luncheon, never to be forgotten for the cordial welcome by both he and Mrs. Douglas and their interesting family, not to say the delicious salmon and other delicacies after shipboard fare."

James Douglas and Edward Cridge were two very different men. They were both, however, strong-willed men of principle, and they formed a bond that day that would last a lifetime and see them through the many challenges to come. They shared common objectives, and although Edward was new to the land, he would grow to love it as Douglas already did.

It was fortunate the Cridges found the salmon Douglas served delicious, because they were to eat much of it in the years ahead. It was a staple at the fort and in the settlement, augmented by deer and fowl, which were readily available to local hunters in the surrounding forests. Mary's great delight was the tea with fresh milk, newly baked bread and butter. It was a wonderful treat after the hard, stale biscuits she had endured at sea. Grain was grown locally and other foodstuffs were imported readily from the mainland. More exotic items such as tea or dried fruits came from Asia or the South Seas.

Mary Cridge's first view of her new home from the deck of the *Marquis of Bute* must have been daunting: odd-looking, rough-hewn log buildings and muddy lanes where animals of many types seemed to roam at large. The close-up view was no better. The fort dominated the settlement, with other small buildings scattered about in a clearing. These formed the crude beginnings of a village that looked as if it had been thrown together without any thought.

The Cridges were provided with rooms in the fort's main building until the parsonage, which was under construction, could be finished. Although the log fort had been built with a palisade and bastions for protection, it was evident that the ramparts would not keep out intruders should there be a serious attack. The uniformed sentries at the gate looked the part but in reality were largely symbolic. The previous year, during war between Britain and Russia, there had been speculation that Fort Victoria might be attacked by ships from Russian-held Alaska. Fortunately nothing happened, for the fort could not have withstood heavy naval guns.

Interior of Fort Victoria: Residence of Chief Factor and Mess Hall on left;
Bachelor Quarters and School Dormitories on right, c. 1860
(BC ARCHIVES, A-04098 / PHOTO: MAYNARD)

Mary Cridge was happy with the large, airy rooms of their quarters.
Even with their log walls and lack of furnishings, the accommodations
were an improvement over the cramped dark cabin aboard the *Marquis*.
A large rat that scuttled across the floor the first night took nothing away
from her relief at finally reaching their destination. Edward later recalled:
"She fairly danced with joy at our release from the long and tedious con-
finement of shipboard."[1] During the first year in the fort the Cridges had
few of the comforts of home as they knew them in England, but they had
faith that the situation would soon improve.

Mary accepted her new situation with equanimity, and did not comment in her diary on how strange she felt in her rough new surroundings.
The optimism and confidence of Douglas were contagious, and she easily
came to share his dream of a magnificent future on the edge of a beautiful
wilderness. Douglas convinced the Cridges that the land was rich with resources and suitable for cultivation, and that it would provide for all their

needs. He also explained that trade was the foundation on which the settlement had begun and bartering with the Natives was well established. The nearby Native camp supplied much of the fort's fish and seafood. Although the smell from outhouses and garbage piles could be overwhelming depending on the direction of the wind, Mary acclimatized quickly and soon became accustomed to confronting the goats, pigs and various other animals that prowled the muddy tracks.

The Cridges knew that the relationship they developed with James and Amelia Douglas would be all-important to their endeavours. After their first meeting, their hopes of success were greatly improved, for they found Douglas to be a devoutly religious man anxious to support a Church of England presence at the fort.

During his time at Fort Vancouver, Douglas had worried not only about feeding and housing his people but also about satisfying their souls. A small, primitive community with only a handful of settlers was not terribly appealing, and he had had difficulties finding a chaplain who would live at the fort and minister to the sometimes rough-and-tumble residents. With a growing family himself, Douglas was well aware of the need for education and Christian instruction.[2] Although Roman Catholic missionaries had been active on the coast for several years, he felt a Church of England minister and a fine church building were essential for the new fort on Vancouver Island.

For Douglas, it was a mixed blessing when the Cridges' predecessors, the Reverend Robert John Staines and his wife Emma arrived at the Vancouver Island colony on March 17, 1849. Staines had graduated from Cambridge in 1845 and was a college friend of Edward Cridge. Although devout, he was an acquisitive, argumentative man, more entrepreneur than pastor. He created problems for Douglas when he promoted a form of representative government that would have reduced Douglas's control of the community.

Both Staines and his wife were also employed as teachers. They had twenty-two pupils when the school opened on the top floor of one of the fort's buildings. Staines, however, was extremely stern with youngsters, a practice typical of the English school system, but one that did not go over well in the new land. One of his students described a session with him as a "day of terror."[3] His wife Emma was the better teacher but was also a strict disciplinarian. Moreover, she refused to have anything to do with the mixed-blood wives of some of the traders whose children attended the school. As a result, both Staines and his wife antagonized many of the colonists. Always dressed strictly in the English fashion, the couple exuded an air of superiority, setting themselves apart from the parents of the children and many members of the congregation at the fort.

Staines had written to Cridge on October 26, 1849, describing life in the colony and explaining his trials and tribulations in trying to fit into a community essentially ruled by one man. He also seemed to live in constant fear of the Natives, the Cowichans and Chilcotins, as he called them. James Douglas's view of Staines was as "a fomenter of mischief and . . . a preacher of sedition."[4] Tension between the two men increased when Douglas recommended to the resident council the appointment of his brother-in-law David Cameron to the Supreme Court of Civil Justice. He claimed the move was needed due to a shortage of qualified candidates, and an earlier appointment of four untrained men as magistrates had proven to be a disaster.

That this was true did little to blunt Staines' charges of nepotism. Increasingly angry, Staines finally led a campaign to get rid of the governor, obtaining considerable support from large landowners such as the Scottish immigrant John Muir, who had arrived in 1849 and became the first successful large business owner in Sooke.

In February 1854, the Douglas-Staines dispute reached the boiling point. Douglas told the minister his position as schoolmaster would end in June. Staines drafted a petition attacking the abilities and character of David Cameron and asking the government to remove him from office. He then signed and circulated a new petition protesting Douglas's appointment as governor of Vancouver Island. Staines readily volunteered to take the petition to England, setting out as soon as possible in winter weather. This was a somewhat headstrong move, and Staines' ship foundered in the Strait of Juan de Fuca, just off Cape Flattery in what was to become Washington State, and all aboard drowned. The petition went down with him, and although John Muir started another petition, the situation changed and it was never sent.

It was in these circumstances that James Douglas had found himself once again in need of a chaplain and, as a result, the Reverend Edward and Mary Cridge came to Fort Victoria.

5

Putting Down Roots

As Edward and Mary adjusted to their new way of life and learned to cope with its peculiarities, they were intrigued by Douglas's unusual practices and the many facets of his responsibility. In the early days Douglas had seen himself as supreme commander of Fort Victoria, and he ran the operation like a military base. He and his men shared meals in a common eating hall and slept primarily in rooms provided for them within the fort. Dinner was a special event usually highlighted by salmon. Although the fish was tasty, there were complaints about there being too much of it, especially when served for breakfast. All of the bachelors, senior officers and company officials ate together, while wives, children and other employees dined in another room. The mess hall had a large fireplace and the table was set with fine linen, china, silver dishes and cutlery. Douglas presided over all.

Dr. J. S. Helmcken, c. 1892
(BC ARCHIVES, A-02844 / PHOTO: HALL AND LOWE)

While he resided in the fort, the Reverend Cridge gave the blessing for the meal.[1] As is normally the case in an army mess, there was much wine and many toasts, always including one to the Queen. The men smoked their pipes and listened to Douglas expound nightly on the history of the Company and on his plans for the future of the colony. Controversy was carefully avoided as Douglas lacked a sense of humour and would brook no criticism. He was respected for his leadership and drive but not particularly loved, and when he left the table to join his family, Cridge noted that the atmosphere in the large hall lightened. Horseplay and singing often carried on into the small hours. Life at the fort was communal, barracks living, and the close proximity of so many people made close friendships inevitable.

Edward and Mary soon met other residents who had rooms behind the stout log walls of the fort, and several became lifelong friends and church supporters. Dr. John Sebastian Helmcken, the Company surgeon, and William John Macdonald, later Senator Macdonald, had arrived a few years earlier. Macdonald's wife was the former Catherine Balfour Reid, the daughter of the Hudson's Bay Company captain James Murray Reid. She became a close confidante of Mary.

Cridge recognized in the doctor a kindred spirit. Helmcken had no dreams of building an estate for himself but wanted a new life in a different kind of world. John Sebastian Helmcken was born in London, England, in 1824. He came to Victoria in 1850 aboard the Hudson's Bay Company's ship the *Norman Morison* and was hired as the Company's first doctor on the coast. Helmcken liked the new settlement and knew there was great need for his services. He became a devoted resident and important asset to the community. In addition to treating most of the early residents, he was physician at the jail for sixty years. His ideals closely paralleled those of Edward and Mary Cridge. Recollecting his first meeting with them, he said, "They were young people and Mrs. Cridge [was] a nice amiable, pretty-looking and slim young lady, but had had no children then."[2]

In the years to come, the doctor was called on many occasions to the Cridge home to assist at the births of their children and treat them when they were sick. He also worked with them to raise funds for Victoria's first hospital and a female infirmary. Helmcken married Cecilia Douglas, one of the governor's daughters, of whom he wrote, "I had soon fallen in love with Cecilia" and "I spent much of my time courting."[3] His commitment to the community and its founding families led him into politics as an elected official. Dr. Helmcken lived to the age of ninety-six, dying in Victoria in 1920. His home, Helmcken House, although not located on the original site, remains a place of interest to visitors.

Another good friend that the Cridges made soon after their arrival was William John Macdonald. Born on the Isle of Skye, Scotland, in 1832, Macdonald arrived on the Pacific coast in 1851. At the age of nineteen he was hired by the Hudson's Bay Company and held a number of jobs in Victoria before he was elected mayor from 1866 to 1867. He was a member of the Reverend Cridge's first congregation in the fort, and a member of the first Board of Education organized by Cridge. Macdonald became a senator on December 13, 1871, on the recommendation of Sir John A. Macdonald. His wife Catherine and Mary Cridge worked closely together on many community projects, most important among them the hospital and the B.C. Protestant Orphans' Home.[4]

By the end of their first week Edward and Mary had met most of the fort's residents, and the new chaplain had carefully prepared his first sermon. The service was well attended, for most Company employees and their families were anxious to put in an appearance and to judge for themselves whether the chaplain was a man of God and someone they could admire. The Reverend Cridge pleased his congregation with a sincere, simple message. He told them: "I am persuaded that it is no chance which has brought me to stand before you today as your minister, or which has caused you to assemble together as a flock committed to my care. I did not leave my former charge, that of a populous district near London, without evident token of the over ruling hand of God." He circumspectly refused to comment upon "the train of events which caused the vacancy which I was called upon to fill."[5] A meticulous man, he carefully filed away his written words, his first sermon in his new home, a habit he was to follow all his life.

He later wrote about these early services: "For over a year service was held at the Fort, whose tall palisades, frowning bastions and sentinel at the gate contrasted with, and even heightened the peaceful nature of the exercises of the assembly within, where newcomers mingled their praises with the devotions of the earlier adventurers."[6] The Reverend Cridge conducted his Sunday morning services in the mess hall during the first year. Dr. Helmcken described it as "twenty feet in length by about a dozen in breadth, lined with upright plank, unpainted.... In the centre stood a large dilapidated rectangular stove."[7] The room was cleaned early each Sunday morning by a group of volunteers in preparation for Cridge's service, a necessary procedure following the bachelors' Saturday night revelry. The mess hall during service was a welcome gathering place in a quiet, contemplative setting for the whole community.

Within a few weeks the Reverend Cridge had demonstrated his commitment to his new way of life and the far-flung area that was his parish, which extended from Colwood and Esquimalt to Sooke, Metchosin, Royal Oak, Mount Newton and as far as Nanaimo, where he travelled by ship. Since there were no roads, he slogged his way, either on foot or horseback, along the few tracks hacked into the forests. He travelled this circuit in summer, when the sun shone brightly, and faced choking dust as the soil dried out. In winter, the rain pelted down and he had to churn his way through knee-deep mud. He was out even when snow was falling. Regularly he begged or borrowed a horse from the fort or a parishioner so he could visit the naval base at Esquimalt and minister to the men there, as well as the growing number of people homesteading along the roads.

Some of the road conditions Cridge contended with are best described in the diary of a young English soldier serving on the Island. Lieutenant Charles W. Wilson endured them in pursuit of pleasure, going to a dance where a few young women were to be found. He described his trip vividly over "roads nearly impassable from the steady rain for days. In the town of Victoria the mud is so deep that it comes up to the horses' girths, and foot passengers can cross only on planks laid across. . . . Outside the town it was much worse . . . on a most dreadful road, if road it can be called at all, the stumps of trees in many places still sticking up in the road."[8]

Edward Cridge encountered similar situations as he ministered to his scattered flock. He married the young, baptized the children, visited the sick and buried the dead, and he also ventured aboard ships in the harbour to carry his message to the seamen who spent their lives afloat.

As Nanaimo began to grow, he found his duties there increasing. In May 1857, as the sole representative of the Church of England in the area, he was the first ordained minister to conduct a regular service in the growing settlement. It was held in Nanaimo's Colonial School House for a congregation that would in later years become the parish of St. Paul's. For the next two years the Reverend Cridge sailed periodically to Nanaimo to conduct these services, but he could not make the trip often enough. In 1859, the Reverend Richard Lowe became the resident Church of England clergyman and continued to use the school as a place of worship. Construction of the first St. Paul's Church was begun on Christmas Day 1861.

In the fort, Mary Cridge set up a school and took her job as a teacher seriously. In one memo she wrote that the work is a "great and good one." She prayed that God would make her "a wise, faithful and diligent teacher."[9] Pledging to be constant and punctual in her attendance, she said she must always remember her class in her daily prayers. Mary also decided to visit the children's homes to cement the bond she was developing with them at the school in the fort and on Sundays. She was gentle but firm with a range of children of many ages, some of whom had never before attended classes. The novelty of the school produced full attendance each week, and her warm sincerity and care soon earned her the respect of the children's parents. The children all regarded her with the same affection as those she had taught in faraway West Ham.

The dedication of both Edward and Mary Cridge quickly convinced Governor Douglas that he had found a minister worthy of his trust. Only a short time after their arrival, Douglas took Edward to the crest of a hill outside the fort and showed him the site chosen for the first Protestant church and cemetery. The large plot, six hundred feet square, was part of the community plan drawn up by Joseph Pemberton. Construction of a fair-sized parsonage, in which the couple and other members of their family could live in comfort, was already underway, and the foundations for the church were laid.

The bishop of Rupert's Land at Red River, head of the Church of England in the West, had recommended the construction of a boarding school for children of the Company's officers as well as a parsonage. Taking a survey to establish the number of children, Cridge found an urgent need for a school for the daughters of Company officers. There were only a few officers' families at the fort and very few sons, but there were numerous daughters, including four from Governor Douglas's family, who were of eligible age and in need of schooling. Reverend Cridge recommended to the bishop and the governor the creation of a school for girls. The young women could board at the parsonage when it was completed, and as soon as his sisters arrived, they could begin teaching the girls. This would provide the Cridges with some additional income as well as introduce a new education program.

Cridge's sisters, Elizabeth and Mary, had sailed from England in July 1855 aboard the *Princess Royal*, and they arrived in Fort Victoria on December 17. Edward rushed to the harbour to greet them as soon as the ship dropped anchor, but as usual it was the following morning before he was able to see them ashore. It was a happy family reunion and Mary, Edward's wife, for the first time met her sister-in-law, Elizabeth, to whom she had written so often during the long voyage around the Horn. They became lifelong friends.

The Reverend Cridge continued to deliver his regular services in the fort while the church was being built on the acreage provided by the Hudson's Bay Company. Edward watched carefully as the building took shape on the land soon to be known as Church Hill. Well outside the fort on the crest of a knoll, it was an inspiring gothic structure, its slender spire stretching into the sky. The parsonage, located on what is now Humboldt Street, was completed in the spring. The four Cridges, along with Mr. and Mrs. Raby and Mary Herbert, were able to move into their first real home in Victoria in April, shortly before the official opening of the church, which was completed in the summer. The parsonage was a big brown two-storey house with extra-large bedrooms that could be used as dormitories for children who boarded there while attending school.

On Sunday, August 31, 1856, a delighted Edward and Mary Cridge attended their first service in the picturesque four-hundred-seat church. For many days they had prepared for the opening of the most significant building in the community. The grand celebration was attended by their close friends James Douglas, Dr. Helmcken and William Macdonald, in addition to all the other parishioners they had met in the fort during the year.

The silver chalice received by the Cridges as a wedding present and other gifts from the congregation added personal touches to the church. It was a proud moment for them all and a milestone in the brief history of Fort Victoria. Edward named the graceful edifice Christ Church in honour of his old parish in West Ham, England. The impressive building gave Edward new stature in the community outside of the fort, as he now became recognized as the resident Church of England minister and the only Protestant preacher. He was no longer seen as just a man employed by the Hudson's Bay Company for the benefit of their employees.

The parsonage was gradually furnished by the Cridges with help from the congregation. Mary had brought with her linen, cutlery and dishes that she was finally able to use, her hope chest collected since she was a young girl in an era when every young woman began preparing for her marriage early in life. Within days the spacious building began to feel a little like home. The move to the parsonage added to the confidence of the congregation that the church and its minister were here to stay, permanent fixtures in the community. Edward's sisters were anxious to begin their teaching duties and settled in quickly, eager to meet their first class of girls, who would board at the parsonage.

Mary Cridge continued to assist with the school and to manage the affairs of the household. Despite the increased workload, Mr. and Mrs. Raby and Mary Herbert were pleased to be responsible once again for the upkeep of a proper home — not just rooms in the fort. They cleaned and polished, made curtains for the rooms, throw-rugs for the floors and sewed blankets for the boarders' bedrooms. They often relied on friends they had met at the fort to tell them the best sources for the goods they needed, be it wool from a local sheep farm or a source of meat for all the mouths to feed.

The way of life in the settlement began to show signs of change shortly after the arrival of the Cridges. Some of the old fur traders and their wives became a little more affluent and adopted more sophisticated ways. The women became more conscious of how they looked at public functions, and the men, at their wives' insistence, learned new dance steps for social events instead of jumping jigs and reels to a fiddler's tune. Young boys took up the game of cricket instead of rough-house games and young girls found enjoyment in dressing up for Mrs. Douglas's picnics.

The parsonage and church became the hub of activity for many residents, and with so many comings and goings, the Cridges quickly became aware of the concerns that occupied the people of their parish. A number of these indicated that the monopoly held over this great expanse of land by the Hudson's Bay Company might soon be at an end.

6

The End of
Company Rule

By the mid-1850s, new arrivals to Vancouver Island wanted a new system of government, something more democratic than the Hudson's Bay Company provided. In just a few short years, Fort Victoria had grown into much more than the trading post of 1849. The standing joke, attributed by some to the Reverend Staines, was that the initials "HBC" for the Hudson's Bay Company meant "Here Before Christ." There were increasingly vocal complaints about the Company's stranglehold on the settlement: the prices it charged for land and goods, as well as its rules and restrictions. The settlement was far from England — and far from every arriving Englishman's cup of tea. Meanwhile, south of the border, a growing number of influential Americans felt the United States should push as far north as they could, despite the 1846 agreement on the forty-ninth parallel.

The colonial office in London, recognizing some of the problems the huge District of Caledonia was facing had taken steps to reduce the power of the Hudson's Bay Company by breaking up its land leases and creating the Colony of Vancouver Island in 1849. In preparation for the future, officials encouraged new enterprises and took steps to increase immigration, putting the settlement at Fort Victoria on the road towards self-government. The Government of Great Britain did not, however, purchase the contract controlling Vancouver Island and the mainland from the Hudson's Bay Company until August 1858, when the mainland also became the Colony of British Columbia. In 1866, the two colonies were combined under Douglas as British Columbia, eventually becoming a province of Canada in 1871.[1]

Because he had been in charge of Fort Victoria since its inception, James Douglas had expected to be chosen as the first governor of the Vancouver Island colony, but Great Britain decided otherwise. It chose instead a governor who was not tied to the Hudson's Bay Company, one who was more cultured and not a mixed-blood fur trader. Unfortunately, he was also ill prepared for the position. To Douglas's chagrin, the government had sent out Richard Blanshard, aged thirty-two, a barrister with no previous experience in colonial administration, who accepted the post without salary. He was a relative of Edward Langford, an influential early settler. Blanshard was appointed to the post in 1849 and arrived in March 1850.

Many years later Cridge reflected that it must have been difficult for both Douglas and Blanshard. Certainly Douglas did not make it easy for Blanshard, who was unhappy from the outset with the remote posting and the degree of control wielded by the Hudson's Bay Company. Douglas was difficult and it was an impossible situation for Blanshard. Douglas especially opposed the scrutiny of his accounts, while Blanshard in turn objected to the manner in which money was given to Native people for their land. He also criticized expenditures made by Douglas for public purposes. Douglas doled out the money and then expected to be reimbursed by the government office.

When settlers submitted a petition for the creation of a governing council for Vancouver Island, Blanshard did not like the idea any more than Douglas but he grudgingly agreed to the idea.[2] However, the request to have Douglas on the council was too much for Blanshard, and eight months after being sworn in with fitting pomp, pageantry and pledges of loyalty, he requested to be relieved of his post. Accustomed to a more genteel lifestyle, he disliked the rough living conditions at the fort and the constant conflict with Douglas. He also found he was unable to build a rapport with the residents. The British government was ill pleased, and the short-term governor found himself paying his own way back to England from San Francisco.

In May 1851, Douglas was officially offered the governorship of the colony of Vancouver Island, although he continued as chief factor of the Hudson's Bay Company. He accepted an annual salary of eighteen thousand pounds. Before long, he sent to England for a proper governor's uniform, which he donned on every possible occasion. He also ordered clothing suitable for a governor's wife. Douglas purchased one hundred acres of land for his own use and began building a home for his family away from the fort. Here he employed Natives after teaching them how to milk cows and harness horses to pull carts. It was difficult for him to change his style of command, and he continued to govern the colony in the same military fashion he had used previously.

The turning point in the form of government came in February 1856, less than a year after the arrival of Edward and Mary, when Douglas received instructions from England to set up an elected assembly. He chafed at the order, not only because it would undermine his authority, but because he felt it would be ineffective. He was sure the creation of a representative system of government under the existing circumstances on Vancouver Island would be only a parody.[3] He explained his feelings to the Reverend Cridge, hoping to enlist his support on the issue. Edward

Cridge did not completely agree with the process but felt it was a beginning; a first step towards more participation in government. Douglas was also opposed to universal suffrage, believing that most people wanted the wealthy "ruling class" to make the decisions. He subsequently set the qualifications for participation in the election so high that, in effect, the wealthy did rule. Douglas established four electoral districts, with Victoria, the largest, entitled to three members on the assembly, Esquimalt two members, and Sooke and Metchosin one each. The only eligible voters were British citizens who owned twenty or more acres of freehold land worth at least three hundred pounds, and so the franchise was restricted to just forty men. Few candidates ran in the first election and only the Victoria seats were contested, the others were filled by acclamation.

The election was quickly and quietly set for July 22. Despite Douglas's aversion to it, the first House of Assembly opened on August 12, 1856, and Edward Cridge gave the opening prayer. Edward was also named clerk of the Legislative Council. The members included Governor Douglas; the surveyor James Pemberton; Joseph McKay, a Hudson's Bay Company employee; Dr. John Helmcken; James Yates from Metchosin; John Muir from Sooke; and Thomas Skinner and Joseph Robertson from Esquimalt. The assembly's inaugural meeting was not the momentous occasion it might have been as the first elected legislature west of the Great Lakes. The men met in a small room in the fort furnished with simple chairs and an old table. The total cost of the meeting, according to Dr. Helmcken, was about twenty-five pounds.

Retired Chief Factor John Work commented on some of the later proceedings, in agreement with Douglas: "I have always considered such a Colony and such a government where there are so few people to govern as little better than a farce...There are too few people and nobody to pay taxes to cover expenses."[4]

* * *

Songhees with "inverted basket" hat
(BC ARCHIVES, AA-00253 / PHOTO: FREDERICK DALLY)

From her first sight of them as the *Marquis of Bute* entered the Victoria harbour, Mary had been concerned about the plight of the Songhees people. She had spotted the smoke rising from their fires in what looked like a particularly squalid group of makeshift shelters and tents on the north side of the harbour. Ever curious, she asked about the people there and learned that these were the Songhees Natives who had moved in and set up a camp while the fort was being built. She felt it was her duty to do something to improve the conditions under which they lived. However, she found this difficult to achieve, despite attempts to explain their needs to those who might be able to help.

Mary found that Native life and the Victorian-influenced lifestyle of the newcomers were diametrically opposed, creating difficulties for Natives and settlers alike. Language was the initial barrier, making direct communication difficult, and misunderstandings were numerous. As more women arrived and families built homes and began to raise children, the clash of cultures became greater. The highly structured life of the Church-centred newcomers was at odds with the unrestricted communal lifestyle of the Natives. There were no easy solutions and the authorities did not seem anxious to respond to Mary's entreaties. The alcohol readily available from the settlers affected many of the six hundred Songhees badly, causing incidents of fighting and stabbing.

Douglas was sympathetic to the Native people and had hired some of them to work on his farm, but they were not trained in the skills necessary for regular employment in the settler community. They preferred to do manual labour only on an irregular basis, but found life generally easier near the colonists, who traded with them for surplus game and fish. When Mary looked to find friends and parishioners to employ Songhees workers they often refused, believing Natives to be lazy and shiftless.

Dr. Helmcken was also sympathetic to the plight of the Native people, and Mary enlisted his aid in improving their situation. Soon after his arrival he found most of the Natives living in "hovels," in what he described as "dirt and filth" along the shoreline above the mudflats.[5] Many had only a blanket for clothing, and apart from trading and occasional manual labour, they seemed to him to idle many of their hours away. He realized that many of the diseases he saw among the Songhees had been brought by the settlers. As he commented, the "waifs and strays" that come to the Northwest brought "religion for saving the soul" but also "diseases destroying the body."[6] Nevertheless he was unable to interest them in his suggestions for improvements in their village.

The governor kept a close watch on the Natives and discussed his concerns with the Reverend Cridge, but they could think of nothing that could be done to improve the situation. Initially there was little crime, but then a cow was stolen and Douglas acted quickly. Private ownership was a concept difficult to explain to the Songhees, who were accustomed to sharing

Old Songhees reserve, c. 1880
(BC ARCHIVES, F-09955)

food and resources. Their camp was a communal settlement. Despite Douglas's best efforts, petty theft increased and was a constant irritant for the new settlers. Other complaints were similar to that of one resident, who demanded action against this "wigwam settlement, with its practices of depravity and vice which are injurious to the morals and business of the city, as well as to the character and best interests of the natives themselves."[7]

Douglas responded calmly, stating that "the presence of the Indians so near the town is a public inconvenience, but their removal would be neither just nor politic."[8] Unfortunately, little changed and animosity festered for decades, the squalor in the settlement a source of disease for the band and a growing concern for everyone else.

The Reverend Cridge, Mary and other religious leaders, particularly the

Wesleyan Methodist missionaries who arrived shortly after Cridge, continued to rail at the situation but little direct action was taken. There was a shortage of church funds, people and resources. The faraway religious authorities were much more concerned with the souls of their congregations than sustenance, and as more religious groups arrived, denominational rivalries diverted attention from the more serious, festering social problems.

7
Education in the Colony

One success for the Reverend Cridge in the years soon after he arrived was the establishment of a local chapter of the Young Men's Christian Association (YMCA). Respect for Queen and country was a major influence on the colony in its early years, and the YMCA, formed in London in 1844, found favour with Cridge. In 1859, the Christ Church minister moved, at a special meeting of local clergy, that the organization be set up in Victoria. It was felt that in an unsettled frontier community there was much to tempt young men.

The YMCA got off to a quick start and opened a reading room on Yates Street, "well supplied with the leading religious publications, and scientific papers and periodicals of Great Britain, the Colonies and the United States." The local newspaper noted the room was a place where young and old could use the facilities to their advantage and spend their leisure evenings. The paper added that it was a healthy check "against dissipation."[1]

The settlement as yet featured few amenities or services for residents. There were no public schools, few communal utilities, no paved roads and no garbage collection. Apart from the odd teacher hired by a group of residents to teach their children, most education was provided by the Church. Like the Reverend Cridge, many ministers were trained first as teachers, because supervision of the church school was an essential part of their duties.

James Douglas was well aware that without a Protestant minister the role of education would fall exclusively to the Roman Catholic Church, and as a governor appointed by the British government, he believed a permanent Protestant presence was essential. This was one of the reasons teaching skills had been a prerequisite for the new chaplain at the fort.

Douglas had not been without spiritual or educational advice on the Island, for Bishop Modeste Demers had been named the first Roman Catholic bishop of Vancouver Island in 1847. He had long been a friend and advisor to Douglas. Bishop Demers was born in Quebec and first moved west to the Red River settlement, in what would become Manitoba, before arriving on the Pacific coast. He was one of the most travelled men in the colony and on the mainland, having visited almost every small community and group of homesteads. He had built a solid reputation and was increasingly admired and respected by those of different faiths and those of no faith at all. Demers had even won the confidence of many Native people he had visited during his long, difficult and often dangerous trips into unexplored territory. He brought some thirty Roman Catholic missionaries to the coast to minister to various Native groups.[2]

Cridge, an ardent believer in education for all, had urged his sisters to follow him to Vancouver Island as quickly as possible so they could take over the operation of a church school. They had been well tutored by their father and were as adept at teaching as their brother. Edward's wife Mary had begun the school upon her arrival but could not continue the task alone, for she had delivered the couple's firstborn shortly after they moved to the parsonage. It was a son whom they named Richard Coombe Cridge. Edward proudly wrote in his diary, "God gave us a first born son, born at one-and-a-half a.m., June 6, 1856." Richard was followed by eight siblings at a rate of almost one per year — not unusual in this era of large families.

As he delighted in watching his new son, the Reverend Cridge became even more dedicated to ensuring that a proper education was provided in Victoria for the mounting number of children. The new legislature in 1856 asked Cridge to form an education committee to inquire into the entire school system, in effect making him the first superintendent of education. Although he received no remuneration, these duties were a labour of love, and he continued to supervise the school system for many years.

Cridge's committee was charged with "enquiring into and reporting upon the state of public schools,"[3] and after its first meeting instructed the Reverend Cridge to administer "quarterly examinations, report upon the progress and conduct of the pupils, on the system of management and all other matters related to the education of children."[4]

Two public schools had been established in the community in addition to the Girl's School at the parsonage. The Victoria School, still located in the fort as it had been when the Cridges first arrived, was now attended only by boys while girls in the town were taught at the parsonage school. In Craigflower, a growing farming community on the Gorge Waterway, those attending included both boys and girls. Another public school had opened at Nanaimo, some sixty miles north, where Robert Dunsmuir and his army of miners from England were establishing a coal mining industry after the discovery of rich deposits that stretched out under the sea.

While Cridge frequently combined travel to visit his parishioners with calls at the schools, the distances involved made the journeys time-consuming and difficult. Visiting Nanaimo meant a voyage up the coast by boat, although this was often preferable to the ride to Craigflower by horse in the rain or snow. Promoting education in the colony had its challenges. Children were not compelled to attend, and some settlers were loath to send them, particularly older children who could be employed working for the good of the family.

Cridge's views on education were well-known. When he had written earlier to officials in England he had emphasized there was a desperate need for a "girl's school for the working class." The now well established parsonage school had been introduced and was under the direction of his sister Elizabeth. Cridge had stressed at the time, "It seems greatly to be lamented that those who are likely hereafter to perform so important a part in the community in the capacity of wives and mothers should be suffered to grow up without education." To many this was a radical view, for the thinking persisted that there was no need to educate girls because their future was foreordained as mothers and homemakers. Needless to say, Cridge's father John had insisted his daughters receive a good education, which enabled them to be hired as teachers. The education of girls was a point the pastor insisted upon during his years as superintendent of education.[5]

Elizabeth was proof that women could become excellent teachers and after some years teaching at the parsonage she gladly accepted more responsibilities as Cridge's assistant in the supervision of education, touring the schools to ensure they were well run. Neither of them received remuneration. Unfortunately, Elizabeth's sister Mary, who had also been trained to teach, found she could not do so. She had been ailing since shortly after her arrival, and soon found she could no longer assist with the school or with household chores. Before long she required continuing care. After several visits and consultation with other doctors, Dr. Helmcken diagnosed Mary with consumption — now known as tuberculosis. The sisters recalled that two passengers on the *Princess Royal* had died, which might have been the source of Mary's illness. Dr. Helmcken said there was almost no hope of recovery and she would be best cared for at home, where she stayed, looked after by her family until her death at age fifty.[6]

Cridge presented his first report to the committee on November 30, 1856. It dealt with only the Victoria and Craigflower schools. He found only seventeen boys between six and fifteen years of age enrolled in Victoria, and he was unhappy with the curriculum because of "the want of accuracy and grounding in the elementary parts." He recalled his own education and wanted something equivalent in his new home. The subjects taught, he reported, included "reading, writing, arithmetic, history, a little geography and grammar."

The Craigflower School included both boys and girls, with twenty-one pupils: eleven girls and ten boys. The Reverend Cridge was pleased with what he found there, stating that the students were "fairly grounded in the elementary parts." Several of the boys had been removed from school for various reasons, including one for immoral conduct, although exactly what that involved was not explained. He noted with pleasure that "improper language" in everyday conversation was becoming rare. Throughout his nine-year tenure Cridge worked consistently to improve the education system. Even after he was no longer in charge, he did his best to ensure the quality of education.

Bishop Demers also took an interest in education, and his stature was heightened in Victoria when, on his recommendation, four nuns were approved by the mother house of the Sisters of Saint Ann at Lachine, Quebec, to come to Vancouver Island in 1858 to open a Catholic school for girls. Its creation and the standards it set played a major role in education for decades to come. The school's aim was to provide a "thorough moral and general education,"[7] and parents of various religious denominations enrolled their daughters. St. Ann's School opened in 1858 in competition with Cridge's own parsonage school, which had opened two years earlier. St. Ann's, however, was better equipped than the parsonage school.

When Demers later opened a school for boys in his own residence, he again was hailed for his contribution to the community. Instruction was to be in two languages, English and French. The newspaper of the day stated that "the school can not but prove to be a great acquisition."[8]

When it became known that the Catholic boys school was to be expanded in 1863, the Church of England, not to be outdone, recommended in 1862 that it construct its own school for boys aged seven and older based on the grammar school system of England. It was open to youngsters for a fee of one hundred dollars a year.

While the Reverend Cridge strongly approved of the school, which he hoped his sons would soon attend, he was involved in an incident that marred its official opening. The chosen headmaster was the Reverend Garrett. Unfortunately, Garrett favoured the harsh discipline that was part of the English public school system, and an uproar developed when the widow of a Captain Dodd protested that her son came home with his legs badly beaten and bruised from a flogging. Opinion was divided, but an editorial in the newspaper maintained that what was described as birching was actually clubbing. Cridge stepped in to mediate, but the paper contended that "through the exertions of the Rev. Mr. Cridge, the matter has been hushed up, and there is, we regret to say, no prospect of a judicial investigation."[9] In fact, there had been no demand for any investigation other than from the editor.

Reverend Cridge oversaw the curriculum and growth of Vancouver Island schools from 1856 until 1865, when Alfred Waddington was appointed as the first paid full-time superintendent of education and the first layman to hold the position, although he would not stay long and resigned after only one year.

8

Gold! Miners Rush In

L ife settled into a comfortable rhythm for the Reverend Cridge and his wife until Sunday morning, April 25, 1858, when the *Commodore*, an American side-wheel steamer from San Francisco pulled into Victoria harbour. Victorians walking quietly home from church gazed in awe at the jam-packed decks of the steamer as it cleared the point and anchored at the pier. It was the largest number of newcomers ever to arrive at one time. Men of every description poured off onto the dusty village streets. They wore red flannel shirts and carried heavy packs and deadly looking bowie knives; many had a revolver openly visible in a holster on their hip. They were a motley group of adventurers with the gleam of gold in their eyes, and they were hell-bent for the mainland, where they dreamed a fortune awaited them. These were the first of the thousands of miners and hangers-on who would pass through the little settlement on their way to the recently discovered Fraser River goldfields.

For the minister and the community fathers, the gold rush of the next few years, first on the Fraser and later in the Cariboo, was a tumultuous time. They knew the visitors would not stay long, but they wondered how the settlement could withstand the onslaught, particularly when liquor flowed freely. One observer noted that problems might soon abound because among the miners were "gamblers, loafers, thieves and ruffians."[1] The Reverend Cridge was well aware of the potential problems. He knew most of the men were seeking gold, not God, but felt he had an obligation to minister to them all. He held outdoor services at the fort for anyone who wanted to attend, and drew a surprising number, as high on some occasions as four hundred — miners as well as others.

The majority of the newcomers were from the United States, and they greatly outnumbered the mostly British residents. Their visits might be short term, but they brought to the fore festering concerns that had until then been held in abeyance. Since the first news of gold in California and Oregon in the 1840s, a considerable number of men had slipped away to try their luck in the south. Many knew that unlike the area under the control of the Hudson's Bay Company, the United States had plenty of free land available. With this recent news of gold along the Fraser River and in the creeks of the Cariboo, Governor James Douglas knew he must contend with a double problem: a new and larger exodus by some of his settlers in search of free land to the south and a major influx from the United States heading for the Fraser River.

It was impossible to tell how many of the newcomers might remain in Victoria for any length of time, but when they came, Douglas, ever the old trader and canny businessman, wanted to capitalize on their presence. He quickly stocked the Hudson's Bay Company's warehouses to meet the anticipated demand. Astute American merchants also moved supplies into the colony, looking for their own bonanza. Most miners had packed as much basic equipment as they could carry, but they still needed food, clothing and tools, along with transport across the Strait of Georgia to the mainland. Men arrived in a steady stream to replace the numbers that daily crossed the strait in every manner of improvised craft. The larger vessels looked the safest, but they often carried three and four times as many passengers as they were designed for, and their holds were jammed with freight for the journey to the interior.

While the men from the *Commodore* did not pack the pews in Christ Church or regularly attend the outdoor services, they moved on quickly and caused little trouble, lessening residents' original fears. Their only objective was to buy provisions and then carry on across the Strait of Georgia to the mainland and travel up the Fraser River. Gold rush fever had infected men of every occupation and trade, and they left their businesses and jobs to join in the hunt. Some tried the overland route from the United States, but with "Indian trouble" in Washington State, the bulk of the gold seekers chose all sorts of small craft to travel up the coast to Fort Victoria. Vancouver did not yet exist. The Reverend Cridge contacted the Colonial Church and School Society back in England, requesting pastors for the mainland where the miners would settle. He asked for two ministers, one for the diggings in the Cariboo and one to assist him in Victoria. But help would not arrive for months. Meanwhile, other denominations were also sending ministers to serve the burgeoning populace of Vancouver Island and the mainland.

Victoria's primitive streets and trails were soon chewed up by the population that had suddenly doubled. A sea of tents and crude shacks appeared around the perimeter of the fort, and the need for lumber sharply increased as two hundred rough-and-ready buildings were thrown up. Muir's sawmill in Sooke as well as the one at the fort could hardly keep up with the demand. When it rained the roads were worse than ever, and drays sank up to their axles. Residents and storekeepers laid down planks to make walking easier, but as Mary pointed out to her family, if you went visiting or to a shop, almost all your clothes then had to be washed. Fresh water was in short supply, and an awful reek wafted from the latrines that had been dug for the newcomers.

Prices for seafood soared and some of the Songhees made a considerable amount of money. Their women sometimes approached the visiting miners to satisfy their needs. The price of building lots soared from fifty and seventy-five dollars to three thousand and more. An American company started the first real newspaper, the *Victoria Gazette*, and the express freight company Wells Fargo moved in. Victoria was suddenly transformed from a sleepy English frontier community to a bustling wild-west town. When several well-dressed ladies of the night with their own views on moneymaking arrived from California, the Reverend Cridge and other community leaders identified new concerns for the permanent residents.

Those first miners who arrived in the spring of 1858 were the forerunners of an estimated twenty-five thousand who passed through Victoria during the Fraser and Cariboo gold rushes. At the peak of the rush, in July 1858, in one ten-day period vessels brought an estimated fifty-five hundred to Esquimalt harbour, the naval base north of Victoria. Most of them stayed only long enough to vie for scarce and overpriced boat transportation. Some tried in desperation to row and paddle their way across the cold, often storm-swept waters of the Strait of Georgia in makeshift craft, hopping from one island to the next. How many drowned in their efforts to reach the mainland is unknown. Others, mostly merchants, stayed in Victoria and established businesses, a few of which still exist.

* * *

The Reverend Cridge was particularly intrigued by one group among the newcomers from California. He wrote in detail about what he described as some "35 men of colour of different trades and callings chiefly intending to settle here."[2] They represented a larger group of blacks who wanted to leave California due to the passage of discriminatory legislation. One of the most egregious clauses prevented them from testifying in court in any case involving whites. Many had moved to California from the American south, away from slavery and fears of a North-South civil war. They were not accepted by their travelling companions, who labelled them "niggers," but Douglas made it clear they would be welcome in Fort Victoria. They arrived in the colony with hopes of a new beginning.

The Reverend Cridge wrote in his diary, "On Monday [April 26, 1859] drank tea at Mrs. Blinkhorn's with my wife. She told us that on the preceding evening she was surprised to hear songs of praise coming from the men of colour who had taken a large room at Lang's the Carpenter and they had spent the Sabbath evening in worship. On the following morning I called on them. They appeared much gratified by my visit." Cridge was pleased when they stated they would not want to form their own church, but would simply join an existing one. He invited them to join Christ Church, which many of them ultimately did. Before leaving he offered a prayer for their well-being.

A three-man advance delegation from the group had also been received "most cordially and kindly" by Governor Douglas. He repeated that they and others from California were welcome to stay and detailed the land they could buy and its price. He and Cridge knew they would not be well received by some Victoria residents — those who had already voiced their objections when Douglas did nothing to discourage Chinese and other non-whites who had already settled in Victoria. But the delegation was pleased with their reception by Douglas and Cridge, and they reported their experiences to their friends on returning to California. Soon after, they sent an official thank you to both Douglas and the Reverend Cridge.

Estimates vary as to how many "men of colour" eventually came to Victoria from California, but about four hundred is a generally accepted figure. However, the warm welcome they had received from Cridge and Douglas was, as predicted, not universal. There were complaints from those who did not want "niggers" moving in or sharing their church pews. A man named Sharpstone, for instance, complained that in church "the Ethiopians perspired" and smelled.[3] The issue developed into a religious debate when the Reverend Cridge, during a Sunday sermon, chastised any who held these views. A new Congregationalist minister, Matthew Macfie, joined the debate, calling Cridge naive to think the newcomers could freely integrate into the community. He argued that, although they should be treated with the greatest humanity and respect, "the Negroes" should have their own place of worship.

Cridge insisted that the question of colour was an "affair of supreme insignificance before the Almighty."[4] In his quiet but forceful way, he said Christianity demanded that the attitude of both Sharpstone and Macfie be repressed. Another Congregationalist minister, William Clarke, supported Cridge's view when he opposed the stand of his colleague. The affair simmered through some angry public debate in the newspaper. Cridge's repeated contention that his church would accept every race in every pew did not sit well with a few members of his own flock, and the most ardent opponents left Christ Church. Still he did not change his convictions.

Racial tension continued to increase in Victoria, sparked by some newly arrived white Americans who brought with them their racist views. One of the black Californians stressed in a letter addressed to the whole community that he and his countrymen had fled "to a country governed by a nation far-famed for justice and humanity." His name was J. J. Moore, and he pointed out that his group had bought land and opened stores to become contributing members of the young community. He stated that he and his friends had come to "build up for ourselves and children, happy homes in the land of the free and home of the brave."[5] They were hard-working and industrious in their undertakings and in their determination to open up new land for agriculture. Possibly this industriousness was part of the problem, for the "people of colour" enjoyed considerable success and may well have sparked envy in the community.

Cridge's policy of mixed-race church seating was not emulated by the owner of one of the colony's small theatres. There was a fight and a street disturbance at the hall when some blacks protested the form of segregation imposed by the theatre owner, who wanted them to sit in a special section. It was not a major rumpus, but nevertheless a setback for the open-to-all concept favoured by Cridge and Douglas.

A few of the black newcomers moved to Saltspring Island, in the Strait of Georgia, where they farmed successfully. Several went to the mainland, and some returned to other parts of the Pacific Northwest after the end of the U.S. Civil War in 1865, which brought with it the abolition of slavery. The number of blacks in the colony continued to dwindle, and Douglas and Cridge could do little in the face of general public sentiment. All the preaching in the world about the brotherhood of man was to no avail, and for many blacks the dream of a new start in a new country gradually faded.

9

A Hospital for Victoria

W hile education was always a prime initiative for Edward, he realized shortly after his arrival that another pressing need for the community was a hospital where Dr. Helmcken and other medical staff could practise. In the early years, Dr. Helmcken had often travelled to Esquimalt to use the operating room there provided by the navy, and he maintained a residence there for this reason. The beginnings of the Victoria hospital were described in a somewhat fanciful story by members of the Christ Church congregation. One day in the fall of 1858, a sick man was found lying on a mattress in the garden at the parsonage. He had been brought there by nameless parties who knew that the minister would know what to do. The sick man was taken in and nursed back to health.

Others in need of medical attention soon followed, and the Reverend Cridge and Dr. Helmcken enlisted the aid of members of the congregation to care for the sick and injured who came to them for help. Soon a care home was rented, a cottage owned by Mrs. Blinkhorn on the corner of Yates and Broad streets. W. S. Seeley, another parishioner, took charge of the cottage as steward, and Dr. Trimble, a newcomer, was appointed medical officer. This was the very beginning of the Royal Hospital, and though small and humble, it is believed to have been the only public hospital north of San Francisco at this time.

In December 1858, the cottage hospital had seven patients under treatment, but the building was little more than a temporary location and the newspaper of the day reported caustically, "The building is unsuited for a permanent Hospital; the walls are so thin that Indians have broken through and stolen the victuals set for the sick."[1] By February 1859, a wooden building had been erected on the Songhees reserve on the site of the former marine hospital used earlier by Helmcken. It had, said Cridge, the "character of the good Samaritan in its constitution." He emphasized that "none will be exempted from the premises and no question asked as to country, creed or colour."[2]

Financing problems plagued the hospital from the outset. Within five months it was about two thousand dollars in debt, and Cridge called on the territorial government to take quick action to pay off the debit. He pointed out that already there had been forty-nine admissions — thirty-one cures, eight deaths and ten patients still in hospital. Representatives at the meeting of the legislative assembly suggested a poll tax or a tax on new arrivals and people passing through, but none of the suggestions was adopted. Douglas appreciated the hospital's problems, and in an effort to help asked its directors to form a board of health. They would set rules for the hospital, aimed at alleviating some of their financing difficulties, and ease the load on the Reverend Cridge. Cridge emphasized to the assembly that he was not promoting any political sentiment but pressing for "speedy consideration of the best ways and means of discharging a great Christian duty." Many supported Cridge in his call for hospital money lest, as one man suggested, people be left to suffer and die on the streets.[3] Government aid, however, was a long time coming.

The hospital eventually moved to the hill on Pandora Street and was still largely maintained through the efforts of those most involved. Their contributions were supplemented by a diminishing supply of public donations raised from church collections, special events and assorted benefits at the theatre. Cridge accepted all donations, despite questioning the appropriateness of contributions from some of the more popular social events. A frivolous man he was not. Men and women donated whatever they could afford, be it money, hours of volunteer time or — as the church women's groups decided — making bandages. Complaints that the hospital was overcrowded and a disgrace to the community continued, the criticism levelled not at Cridge and his hospital board but at the government for not stepping forward with the necessary funding.

An unusual patient Cridge often visited was Thomas Fraser Campbell, who had played the pipes for the charge of the Highlanders at the Battle of Waterloo. He was reportedly suffering from paralysis. "His downward path to the silent tomb will be smoothed by every attention," said one ardent reporter.[4] The old soldier, however, left on his own terms. Cridge noted that he managed to slip quietly out of the hospital one night, and his body was found some months later in the woods.

As the hospital's debt continued to increase, Cridge called again for public donations, desperately needed because of the governing assembly's continued failure to provide funding. He tried every angle he could think of, including asking for help through stories in the newspaper. He made a special appeal to miners, even those only passing through Victoria, stressing that 30 percent of the patients in the first three years had been miners. He argued that sacred laws held that a portion of everyone's wages belonged to the sick and afflicted. The miners did not buy the proposition. But something had to be done if the policy originally established by Cridge and Helmcken — of never refusing treatment to anyone — were to continue. The newspaper noted that it was an "onerous, unpleasant and thankless"[5] task to try to run the hospital.

A year or two passed before the minister of Christ Church was finally able to report to the hospital board that sufficient money was coming in to set up a women's ward. This had been identified as the most urgent new requirement for the hospital. Mary Cridge took this on as her own special project, raising funds for the much-needed addition. She organized a group of women called the Ladies' Association for Support of a Female Hospital. Both she and Edward's sister Elizabeth were leaders of the organization.

Pregnant women at this time did not receive any prenatal care and little assistance with childbirth. From personal experience and discussions with Dr. Helmcken, Mary Cridge knew a good deal about the subject and some of the complications that could arise. Edward also wrote that there were some women "whose domestic ties did not permit of their being reached by the hospital."[6] In other words, these women went into labour and had their children at home, unattended by a physician. Some of the babies survived but many died. Mary and Elizabeth subsequently developed a new service so that medical attention could be taken to them. Theirs was in essence the first visiting health and midwifery service in the Victoria area.

Through their joint efforts, a maternity ward was also finally established as part of the hospital on Pandora Street. Later it remained a part of a new hospital premises. In 1890, the new hospital was named the Royal Jubilee in honour of Queen Victoria's Golden Jubilee of three years earlier. The old building became a home for the mentally ill.

10

Two Important Newcomers

The Reverend Cridge's request for ministerial assistance from the Colonial Church and School Society was finally answered before the end of 1858.[1] The first to arrive was the Reverend James Gammage, a roving missionary who visited coastal Native communities and mining camps and reported back to Victoria every few months. Cridge's need for a second minister was answered in December 1858 with the arrival of the Reverend William Burton Crickmer, along with his wife and child. They disembarked in Esquimalt and then made their way over the rough road to the parsonage in Victoria, arriving on Christmas Day, much to Edward's delight. The Cridges welcomed the family warmly into their home. For Mary it was a pleasure to have another young mother to chat with and share household duties. The Crickmers remained at the parsonage until the location of the second Church of England in the colony was decided.

The Reverend Cridge took his new colleague to the mainland so they could choose the location together. Because the population was growing and settlement was always changing due to the gold rush, they needed to familiarize themselves with the current state of the land and the small, scattered communities that were appearing along the Fraser River. Cridge planned the journey for early in the year and asked the Reverend Gammage to act as their guide, for he was already familiar with the route to the Cariboo and the town of Barkerville. Gammage agreed to take the two men along for at least part of his next trip.

First they travelled by ship to New Westminster, at the mouth of the Fraser River, and then they followed the rough track that led through the valley and into the canyon as far as Lillooet. Cridge knew well the tidy fields, gentle rolling hills, majestic forests and slow-moving rivers of England, but this new world astounded him. He was amazed by the unending giant trees, the steep mountains that rose sharply into the sky, the roaring rivers with their impassable rapids and the abundance of large wild animals. The threesome travelled long distances in which they saw no one, and whenever they ventured away from the Fraser River, Cridge and Crickmer were awed by the huge trees that blocked out the sun's rays and surrounded them in an eerie silence.

Cridge was the oldest of the three ministers but he must have been in good physical shape, for he and his colleagues made a round trip of several hundred miles over rough terrain — by horse, canoe and on foot — and he enjoyed it all. He and Crickmer learned to paddle a canoe, which they had never done before, and everywhere they went they were welcomed by isolated settlers, some of whom had not seen a minister in years. They spent nights rolled in a blanket, sleeping in a makeshift tent, primitive hut or some other meagre shelter, and shared the humblest of meals with those they met along the route. The Reverend Cridge particularly enjoyed the freedom to conduct the simple evangelical services he loved, and which were so appropriate for the small settlements.

Upon their return, Cridge and Crickmer decided that the site of the second Anglican church in the colony should be at Fort Langley. It was named St. John's.

* * *

Meanwhile, back in England, the letter originally written by Cridge appealing for missionaries and a minister to assist with the work of the Lord on the Pacific coast was read by a Church of England philanthropist, Angela Burdett-Coutts. A wealthy member of a banking family, she had already paid for bishoprics in Africa and Australia and decided that she should do the same for British Columbia. Her decision would have far-reaching effects on the future of Cridge's Christ Church.

A friend of the heiress, the Reverend George Hills, vicar of Great Yarmouth, was named bishop of the newly created diocese of Columbia by the Church. His first function was to undertake a fundraising tour of parishes in England, encouraging congregations to subscribe for his new diocese on the Pacific. His efforts added considerably to the twenty-five thousand pounds Miss Burdett-Coutts had already pledged for a bishop and two archdeacons in British Columbia.

The response to the Reverend Cridge's plea for assistance was a great deal more than he had anticipated. A letter from the Church of England in London arrived in Victoria in July 1859 saying that the Church was very interested in this part of the world and would expand its influence there immediately. He was informed that the Reverend George Hills had been named the first bishop of the new diocese of Columbia, had been consecrated in Westminster Abbey, and could be expected on the Pacific coast early in 1860. The announcement was a complete surprise. It is unlikely that Cridge ever thought a bishop was an immediate necessity in Victoria or that he might have been considered for the position. In any case he did not mention any disappointment at this turn of events in his diary.

Born in Eythorne, near Dover, in 1816, Bishop Hills was only a year older than Cridge. He was ordained in 1840 and served as vicar of Great

Yarmouth, Norfolk, for eleven years. During his career he had the opportunity to study modern parish management and became more of a clerical, political clergyman than Cridge. He cultivated friends among the wealthy in his parish and, most importantly, had impressed Miss Burdett-Coutts. He was elated with his promotion to bishop, believing that this was the first rung on the ladder to even bigger things. He was a tall, handsome man, about six feet four inches in height, with chiselled features, a powerful voice and a full shock of hair silvering at the temples. As the Reverend Cridge would come to know, Bishop Hills generally got along with parishioners and clergy but could be short-tempered when opposed.[2]

* * *

In 1858, before Bishop Hills' arrival on the West Coast, an outspoken newcomer arrived in Victoria, destined to cause considerable trouble for many of the prominent figures in the community. Amor De Cosmos had a profound influence on the young colony, and also caused days of frustration for the Reverend Cridge, the governor and the new bishop. There had been howls of laughter in the legislature of the new state of California some years earlier when a Nova Scotia–born man applied to have his name changed from William Alexander Smith to Amor De Cosmos, which Smith explained meant "order, beauty, the world, the universe."

The controversial new settler founded the community's first regular daily newspaper. Despite his often odd behaviour and some radical views, De Cosmos was a good salesman and later became premier of the province for a short time. This strange "lover of the world" enjoyed theatrical posturing and was often outspoken and argumentative. Born in 1825, he left school at the age of fifteen. How he earned a livelihood before heading west and arriving in Victoria was never explained, but he seemed to have some wealth. He was secretive and delighted in making a mystery of himself. Never married, he lived for a long time in Victoria's Royal Hotel.[3]

De Cosmos's newspaper did not bring in much money in its earliest days, but it made him well-known, and opinions varied throughout the colony as to whether he was famous or notorious. He took an immediate dislike to Douglas and by association to the Reverend Cridge and the Hudson's Bay Company, and he railed against them at every opportunity. In an attempt to state his views more publicly, he launched his four-page sheet, the weekly *British Colonist*, on December 11, 1858, though he had not been a writer or a publisher prior to his arrival in Victoria. It was printed on the press that had produced the very short-lived *Courier de la Nouvelle Caledonie*, a French-language paper sponsored by Bishop Demers that had appeared only twice. Altogether some twenty newspapers were briefly published in Victoria's early days. The *Daily Colonist*, as De Cosmos's newspaper later became known, long outlasted them all. With some name changes and mergers, the newspaper carries on today.[4]

Like most newspaper publishers of his day, De Cosmos had no qualms about slanting the news to his own way of thinking. The writing was frequently outlandish and abusive. He could be vicious, venomous and vituperative, and that was on the good days. His views were espoused in almost every edition, and De Cosmos touted his paper as totally independent. Its four principal objectives were the union of Vancouver Island and the mainland, representation in the imperial parliament in London, construction of a proper wagon road on Vancouver Island, and erection of a telegraph line to connect eastern Canada with the far western colony. The paper carried a mélange of stories from around the world, with emphasis on news from England and its expanding empire. It relied heavily on advertising, which it sold successfully — much of it touting pills and medicines claiming to cure every imaginable complaint. The first printing was two hundred copies and, other than a few local items, all the news was days and weeks old, gleaned from newspapers brought to Victoria by visiting ships.

De Cosmos knew there was considerable support for more democratic rule, and he was nothing if not persistent. Subscribers became used to denunciations such as one describing Douglas's elected representatives as "vain, puffed up, tyrannical, corrupt, short-witted, conceited mummies and numbskulls."[5] Even those who did not support his views were amused by his wild rants. He and his paper weathered many storms. Once, after Douglas demanded a special business performance bond from him in an attempt to shut him down, De Cosmos called an outdoor meeting and asked the public to put up eight hundred pounds. He did raise the money, although probably not all of it from the spectators. The audience laughed on another occasion when De Cosmos was marched through the streets to the government offices, where he was forced to retract what were labelled "incorrect charges." He did, but then denounced the councillors responsible in fine style. They did not call him back for another apology.

He was Douglas's implacable foe: hurling insults, accusations and charges throughout the five years he owned the paper. While he hated the Hudson's Bay Company and Douglas, De Cosmos also generally disliked most of the Island's better known citizens, government officials, military men, professionals and businessmen, although some of them were from time to time his allies. He often changed sides in an argument if the notion took his fancy, and on occasion he even supported his foes Douglas and Cridge.

For himself, Douglas had mixed feelings when De Cosmos announced in 1859 that his paper was expanding and that it would now come out three times a week. The paper included more local news than in earlier days, including much useful information. One story in January 1859 was typical: it announced the arrival of a consignment of silver coins in twenty-, ten- and five-cent pieces and went on to explain for newcomers the colony's monetary system. The system was confusing, using British pounds as well as dollars from eastern Canada and also eventually the American ten-dollar gold "Eagle."

On its third birthday, the *Colonist* congratulated itself, claiming that its circulation for 1861 was over four thousand, nearly all sold on the streets of Victoria. Its importance over the years as the only regular source of news and views in the colony cannot be overemphasized.[6] The *Colonist* became a significant feature of early Victoria, and some of its biggest stories in these years involved the Reverend Cridge and his church.

11

Changes for Church and State

A major concern for the Reverend Cridge just before the new bishop's arrival was inadvertently brought to everyone's attention by Governor Douglas. A long debate took place when the governor sought to have the colony assume the chaplain's costs. Cridge's contract had run out; he was no longer an employee of the Hudson's Bay Company, and money from the colonial office was no longer forthcoming. A further complication was that the land on which Cridge's church and parsonage sat did not belong to the Church. Douglas had originally provided one hundred acres as a glebe to the minister. The Company land was intended to provide money for the church and the Reverend Cridge from farming, but it proved to be unproductive. Douglas had then provided one hundred pounds annually to cover the cost of provisions for the parsonage. The governor's proposition to council was to increase these funds through a grant.

The request led to bitter charges that this would create a state-funded church. Some settlers opposed the payment on religious grounds, because they belonged to other denominations; others opposed it on principle because they had developed a dislike for the Hudson's Bay Company. Many were opposed because the initiative would require increased taxes. Amor De Cosmos carefully mounted a new campaign opposing a state church.

Quietly watching the debate was Modeste Demers, the Roman Catholic bishop at Victoria, who for years before the Reverend Cridge's arrival had been the only well-established religious leader in the colony, although he had never been paid by the Hudson's Bay Company. He raised no complaint about the proposal that would give the Church of England new status and funding that was not available to him. The priest was astute enough to know that he could remain on the sidelines, because others already opposed an official state church.

Douglas again raised the issue of Cridge's salary in September 1859 and asked that four hundred pounds be paid annually. De Cosmos jumped on the issue and charged that such a move would be "an injustice to Roman Catholics" and other religions, and that it would create dissension and bigotry instead of harmony in the community. His newspaper trumpeted, "No state church shall ever be allowed to exist on Vancouver Island."

Members of the colony's assembly, whose days were numbered in any event due to a forthcoming election, looked at De Cosmos's complaint briefly before adroitly handing the issue back to Douglas. The governor in turn extended Cridge's stipend for six months, knowing that at the end of this time the issue would be a problem for the colony's second elected government. With his five-year contract about to lapse, the Reverend Cridge took the issue into his own hands and wrote to England, to the colonial secretary, the Duke of Newcastle, explaining that his contract was expiring and that he desperately needed funds to continue his work. This was one of the key issues that awaited the arrival of Bishop George Hills, described sardonically by some as "the very model of an Anglican prelate."[1]

Bishop Hills arrived in Victoria in January 1860, making an unusually quick journey from England because it was no longer necessary to travel around Cape Horn. A railway had been built in Panama to span the isthmus between the Atlantic and Pacific oceans on the same route the canal would eventually take. It was fortunate that Hills changed his travel plans in San Francisco and cancelled passage on the steamer *Northerner* in order to take a larger ship up the coast. The *Northerner* was wrecked en route, with a loss of forty lives.

Bishop Hills' commanding and formal appearance worked against him from the moment he arrived in Victoria. To some, George Hills conveyed the impression of a Church of England aristocrat, his quiet, sure confidence conjuring up visions of ancient churches and abbeys, elaborate ceremonies and the crowning of England's kings and queens. He was admired for his position, yet in the frontier community he was labelled as a snob, perhaps unfairly, by long-term residents who had struggled physically with the difficulties of daily life. In short, Bishop Hills found it difficult to fit into the still rough-and-ready community, and he also became an easy target for De Cosmos.

The Reverend Cridge read the official welcome when he spoke at a well-attended reception held in the bishop's new residence. The house had been months in preparation, paid for by some of the funds that Hills had raised in England. Located on Fort Street, it was not far from Christ Church. The Reverend Cridge expressed thanks that Hills had not been aboard the *Northerner* and read the welcome printed on a parchment signed by hundreds of local residents. He said Hills would appreciate the vitality of the Church in the colony, and that the residents had received with great pleasure the bishop's plans for the formation and maintenance of schools. Cridge added that this was "a benefit which we are rejoiced to find will be extended to the Indian race."[2] With such a shortage of funds for education, Natives had not previously been encouraged to attend local schools, although Roman Catholic missionaries taught in some Native communities.

Cridge subsequently explained to the bishop some of the important local issues, among them the payment of his own salary and the ownership of the property on which Christ Church stood. Consequently, one of the bishop's first acts was to put to rest De Cosmos's accusations that there would be an attempt to create a state church. He stated proudly that the Church of England expected no funds from government or any exclusive privilege from the state. They would raise their own money and would be self-sustaining. He proclaimed: "We ask only for liberty, a fair field and no favour."[3] As proof of his intent, the bishop returned two outlying pieces of land to the colony, land that Douglas had recently provided to Cridge for the construction of new churches. The bishop added that he would provide the necessary funds to support all his churches and the ministers in his diocese from his sponsor, the Society for the Propagation of the Gospel. An agreement signed by all parties required Cridge to give up the Hudson's Bay Company's hundred-acre glebe around the church, which would be replaced by twenty-five acres, in order to accommodate Christ Church, the church hall, parsonage and school, a trade-off agreed to by the governor and the bishop. Three trustees were then quickly nominated to manage the Church-owned property: the governor, Bishop Hills and the archbishop of London.

The Reverend Cridge must have heaved a sigh of relief and once again accepted with enthusiasm the wide-ranging demands on his time, including helping to raise his growing family. The couple's second child, Edward Scott Cridge, was born in 1857. He was followed soon after by their first daughter, Mary, born in 1860. The uncertainties surrounding the minister's salary and the ownership of church lands had been serious concerns for the Cridges. They wanted more stability for their family, and to this end Reverend Cridge put a down payment on a three-acre piece of land in James Bay that he hoped someday would become a home for himself and his family. Although it would be a number of years before their home was built, he named the property Marifield, in honour of his wife, Mary.

The bishop's arrival brought with it many changes. He promptly declared his intention to spend considerable time on the mainland, while maintaining his headquarters in Victoria. He also announced that he had ordered a prefabricated metal building to be used as his own parish church in the colony. It cost twenty-four hundred pounds, and its purchase was made possible by the donations he had raised in England. Erected not far from Christ Church, it was officially named St. John's but was quickly dubbed "the Iron Church." It was demolished in the early 1900s, and ironically the site was then reacquired by the Hudson's Bay Company for a new department store.

Bishop Hills soon set out on his promised exploration of the huge land mass that was his diocese on the mainland. It was an arduous trek by foot, horseback and canoe, similar to the journey Cridge, Crickmer and Gammage had previously undertaken. Like Cridge, Hills was not an outdoorsman by any stretch of the imagination, but he gamely endured the hardships and dangers along the roaring rivers and in the dense forests and mountains. He slept on the ground and in tents and crude cabins, sometimes subsisting on hardtack, very different from anything he had eaten in England. The bishop went out of his way to visit people who lived in scattered, lonely clearings, covering a distance of several hundred miles. He wrote in his diary of his worry that the somewhat mixed population had "lost its British habits and feelings."

When he returned to Victoria, Hills commented in his diary: "Most people have expressed their opinion that I am looking altered from the effects of this journey. I certainly have had a rougher time than I have ever experienced and I have had to do some amount of hard physical labour. My dress has become tattered, my shoes worn out and my appearance anything but clerical. I was in a coloured woollen shirt, no waistcoat, no neck cloth and my coat was in holes. Yet I enjoyed my journey very much."

The Reverend Cridge and Bishop Hills established a friendly relationship at the outset. The bishop was a frequent dinner guest at the Cridge home and stood up in September for the christening of their daughter, whom they named Mary Hills after her mother and the bishop who christened her. That same month the Reverend Cridge was officially designated

The Reverend Edward Cridge

rector of Christ Church by Hills, a rite which to some seemed superfluous but was in the bishop's eyes essential to establish his position as the head of the Church of England in the colony. A lifelong diarist, Hills spent much of his time recording his experiences and writing reports. His diary for 1860 is made up of four hundred handwritten pages that explain much about the man. It also shows that in his first years in the colony he appreciated the work of the Reverend Cridge. He notes, "I am very fortunate in Mr. Cridge, the original chaplain here. He is a truly good man, a sincere and devout Christian. He enters into all my plans and is a great support to me."

The bishop unveiled sweeping expansion plans for the Church. He encouraged Cridge to add new Sunday evening services at Christ Church, and the first collection was earmarked for Edward's favourite project, the hospital. Some sixty pounds went into the plate that evening. "This would be respectable even in Old England," noted the bishop in his diary. Hills met with various other religious and civic leaders in Victoria. After his session with Bishop Demers, of the Roman Catholic Church, he wrote: "I told him I trusted socially we should meet as persons but that our religious differences were fundamental. ... This need not prevent mutual respect as members of the same community. He assented and said this was all he desired."

Despite his assurances to all that he had no ambitions for a state church, Hills continued to have trouble with De Cosmos, who demanded that the twenty-five acres given to Christ Church be returned to the colony. De Cosmos repeated the same story week after week. Unused to this kind of treatment, the bishop complained in his diary that his first four months in Victoria were "more vexatious and troublesome than in all my ministerial life before." And the situation was only to get worse.

Residents of the colony awaited with some interest the upcoming election, though it was not much more democratic than the sham in 1856 because the stringent property and financial requirements still ruled out many people. But this time there were more men on the voter's list than previously. Women still did not have the vote. De Cosmos trumpeted his key election issues: amalgamating with the mainland and joining the Canadian federation. The Songhees, however, were the hot topic with everyone else during the campaign. A majority of the population held Douglas responsible for the Native troubles. In particular, they disliked the instructions he gave for laying out reserve lands; he told the surveyors "to include in each reserve the permanent Village sites, the fishing stations, and Burial grounds, cultivated land and all the favourite resorts of the Tribes...."[4] The settlers argued these guidelines gave the Native peoples too much. They also accused the Songhees of not utilizing the resources well.

The antagonism towards Douglas about his treatment of the Natives had some basis in fact, as Douglas treated Natives more fairly than most of his contemporaries. Yet the settlers were wrong about his being "soft" on the Natives. Douglas moved quickly when the schooner *Royal Charlie* was fired on as it sailed past the Songhees camp on leaving the harbour. The governor advised the Natives to evacuate women and children from the settlement before he moved in with the town's newly formed police force, backed up by a detachment of Royal Marines. Nobody was hurt in the incident, but several of the Native shooters were identified and arrested. They received thirty-six lashes and two months in jail, with the punishment meted out by sailors from Esquimalt. In addition, some one hundred muskets and knives were seized from the Native camp.

De Cosmos's new topic arose principally from the island colony's electoral setup. Editorials in the paper argued that paid lackeys of the Hudson's Bay Company would have the interests of the Company more at heart than those of the people, and that "votes have been bargained for and money paid."[5] Although he had probably intended to do so all along, De Cosmos said he finally found it "imperative to run in the election in the face of such perversion of fair voting."[6] In the end, he and his supporters did not have enough strength at the polls; he placed third in his riding, with only the first two going to the assembly. De Cosmos's political ambitions were put on hold, but in the meantime he continued to voice his views strongly in the *Colonist*. Douglas, Cridge and now Hills continued as his favourite topics.

After the election, rivalry mounted between Victoria and New Westminster over which city would be named the capital when the two colonies united, a long-awaited event. The people of Victoria and their advocate De Cosmos took a "we were here first" approach. They were confident they would win, arguing that they had more government infrastructure than the growing mainland city. New Westminster, in turn, boasted it had a more cultured lifestyle. Victoria countered that it had its own three-year-old philharmonic society.

As the community of Victoria grew, so did the incidence of crime, and the Reverend Cridge's far-reaching role extended to the justice system. One of his most difficult tasks during these years was to offer consultation and the last rites to criminals sentenced to death. The worst incident he recalled occurred in August 1860 and concerned Allache, a twenty-year-old Tsimshian from Fort Simpson, who was sentenced to die on the gallows for the stabbing death of a man named Thomas Brown. It was the tragic end to a dispute between a Native and a black man. Despite considerable public opposition and an eighty-name petition begging for leniency submitted to Governor Douglas, the latter rejected any alteration of the verdict.

On the night before his execution, Allache wept, telling the minister he regretted his crime. Cridge spent hours talking to the young Native in his cell, trying to calm him. When the jailers, who had grown quite fond of Allache, came to say goodbye, he cried again. Accompanied by the minister, who counselled him to his final hour, he was able to walk steadily to the gallows. A curious, silent crowd of about three hundred, many of them Natives, had gathered to watch while armed police stood by in case of trouble. The gallows had been hurriedly erected by Sheriff Naylor and might have served the purpose, but the executioner had never hanged anyone before, and the event became a horrible spectacle.

No one on the police force or jail staff was prepared to be executioner, so a criminal sentenced to work on the chain gang volunteered to do the job in exchange for fifty dollars and his freedom. But the knot on the noose he made, intended to break Allache's neck when he dropped, causing instant death, did not do so. As a result Allache slowly strangled to death.

Cridge was appalled to see him struggling convulsively at the end of the rope for long, tortured minutes. The crowd watched in horror, but the *Colonist* noted somewhat tepidly: "He passed away, we trust, to the happy hunting ground of the Great Spirit."[7]

Cridge had long been a prominent advocate of social reform, and after his unhappy experiences with Allache, he became highly critical of the deplorable conditions of the jailed prisoners in Victoria: "There is no doubt that the accommodation of the prison is insufficient for the criminals, to say nothing of the maniacs."[8] He called on both the government and the public to help with the situation but, as with most such issues, changes were slow in coming.

12

The Bishop's Blunder

I t was at this time that a crisis occurred, irreparably damaging Bishop Hills' reputation with the whole community. The affair arose when some private correspondence written by the bishop to his superiors in London became public knowledge. The incident would haunt him throughout his entire tenure on the Pacific coast. It was De Cosmos who broke the story when, on October 11–13, 1860, he reprinted a report from another paper.

The blunder was exposed innocently enough when newspapers in London carried excerpts from a report Hills had sent to the archbishop of the Church of England describing his first months in British Columbia. It had been intended as a report that would assist in fundraising. Hills had assumed it was a private correspondence and probably never dreamt his comments would find their way into the newspapers. The people of England, however, craved news from the colonies, and everything from the hinterlands was read avidly. Unfortunately for him, Hills' report of life on the frontier was picked up in Canada, travelling all the way to Victoria, where De Cosmos gleefully gave it top billing. All would have been well if Hills had kept to general comments and not added the final paragraphs to his report.

The bishop began the report with words of praise: "Victoria must be, I think, the most lovely and beautifully situated place in the world."[1] He liked the climate, which he found much like England's. He waxed lyrical about lakes, noble forests, sublime mountains and undulating park-like glades. Hills marvelled at trees three to four hundred feet tall felled by men with axes making one pound a day. He wrote poetically of branches waving convulsively as a tree fell: "and then the giant is still, and the vacant sky is seen through where for ages he has proudly stopped the light and warmth of heaven's orb from the earth beneath." He explained that the country was wild for a person used to the gentle English countryside, and he commented on how he had gamely travelled hundreds of miles visiting those who lived in isolation. They, like the country, were a rugged lot, he said, many not able to practise their religion because of the isolation, but happy to see people from the outside world.

Hills went on to make some sound housekeeping points and cost-of-living illustrations. Some things in the colony were cheaper than in England, he reported, and some more expensive. Like the Cridges, he had brought a married couple with him, and he noted that his servants bought good beef and mutton for ten pence a pound, tea and butter for two shillings, sugar for four pence, and potatoes and flour for about the same as at home. Clothes were expensive, and it was difficult to get servants, which meant "having to labour with one's own hands." He emphasized that the colony suffered badly from a shortage of women. Hills recommended that fishermen should be encouraged to migrate to the West Coast, for there was a bright future in the herring industry, where fish could be cured for export. He also saw the possibilities of marketing sturgeon and salmon, emphasizing that the latter was excellent and cheap.

In the report, he praised the Reverend Cridge, saying he "is an excellent good man, but has been burdened overmuch with work. Consequently, Dissenting Chapels are rising up." He cited the Methodists and Congregationalists, and noted the increasing number of Catholic priests and nuns. The bishop indicated that there were too many mediocre preachers who could not get on in England wanting to go abroad. He had a low opinion of many of the ministers he had met on his travels, pointing out that a missionary had no business being in the colonies if he were not a good preacher.

He then gave his opinion on the politics of the region. He said that the Americans in the colony hoped to get enough sympathizers into office at the election to form a majority and push for annexation to the United States. This was an uninformed, inaccurate observation and an insult to many residents. Although it had been clear before they went to the polls that many were hoping for change, becoming part of the United States was not a popular option. Bishop Hills added that Americans did not want black people in the same church with them, but this was again only partly true. He went on to suggest that since there were many Chinese in Victoria, it would be possible for the Church, if money allowed, to take advantage of this fact. It could, he said, "train up natives of that vast heathen people, who will carry the lamp of truth on from our infant Church to the Eastern nations." Hills seemed unaware that many Chinese immigrants wanted to stay in the country.

By far the most damaging and long-lasting effects of his report, however, were his references to Bishop Demers, with whom he had formerly seemed to be on cordial terms. In his letter to England, Bishop Hills now claimed Demers was not pleased with the warm reception Hills had received when he arrived. He then assumed most Roman Catholics voted against the government and added, "I imagine he has incensed his people against me." He direly predicted he would likely "have trouble from the Romanists." Hills also seemed to feel that Roman Catholics had little presence in the colony. But in fact Roman Catholic priests had been among the first to venture onto the coast. Father Jean-Baptiste-Zacharie Bolduc had come to Victoria with Douglas's first expedition, and Bishop Demers had spent a decade travelling Vancouver Island and the mainland.

Hills did recognize that Catholics were, in his words, "forward in the matter of education." They were the only ones, he said, "engaged in the education of girls of the better classes," referring to the much respected St. Ann's in Victoria, which provided a full range of subjects to the high school level. The parsonage school, by comparison, catered only to young girls. On this score he was irritated to find that even members of his own church were sending their children to St. Ann's. He noted that the Church needed to match this "in order to prevent the sapping of the very life-blood of the future population with unsound religion and infidelity." It was this last word "infidelity" that particularly antagonized Bishop Demers and also angered many non-Catholics who were sending their daughters to St. Ann's. De Cosmos recognized a serious misstep by a man he did not particularly like, and he happily reprinted the entire report as it was carried in the English papers.

The Reverend Cridge, aghast at the bishop's sentiments, did his best to repair the damage the article had caused to Bishop Hills and to the Church of England. In an attempt at fence-mending, an exercise probably orchestrated by the bishop, Cridge wrote a letter to Hills, a copy of which he gave to the *Colonist*, where it was printed. It stated that whatever the circumstances under which the report had been written and published, "it does not represent the present opinions of your lordship."[2] Cridge wrote that he felt a word of explanation from the bishop was necessary for people who had aided in advancing the material interests of the colony, including those Americans who had joined with the British to further common goals. The letter seemed to indicate that upsetting the Americans was the biggest of the report's blunders. Cridge wrote that he hoped he would be excused for putting himself in the position of mediator but was confident there would be a restoration of the cordiality that had been upset. This confidence, if such it was, was seriously misplaced, for Hills' comments would long continue to rankle.

Hills' reply to Cridge, which the *Colonist* also carried, was more an excuse for the public release of the report than for the sentiments expressed. Hills noted that the wording of a private communication was not always as carefully done as one intended for publication. The bishop blamed bad information for his annexation views, magnanimously declaring that even friends could not always be expected to be free of criticism. He waffled completely on his statements about Bishop Demers, saying he did not feel the extracts explained his points correctly. The bishop added that he had written to Demers expressing his regrets for any imputation concerning the feelings of the Roman Catholics towards their Christian brethren. He hoped irritation would not cloud the grand objective, which was to "labour in their respective spheres for the common good and to advance the glory of God." In conclusion, Hills said that he trusted Demers would accept his assurance that the imputation was published without his knowledge. He added, "My earnest desire is that nothing lower than the standard of the Charity of the Gospel should rule among us."[3]

On October 16, Bishop Demers response was printed in the British Colonist where he responded to the "slanderous accusations brought against me by Rt. Rev. Bishop Hills." Demers stated he was as loyal a British Subject as any. He also made much of the fact that his churches were supported by the Association for the Propagation of the Faith which received voluntary contributions of one cent per week from Catholics around the world. Hills had spoken in Liverpool during his tour to raise funds and had said, "Nothing had been done for Christianity in these colonies." This had particularly incensed Demers who listed the Catholic Church's long history in North America along with his own early arrival in 1846 as proof of their presence long before Hills arrival only a few months earlier.

A Wesleyan spokesman, meanwhile, countered Hills' claims about the predominance of the Church of England in the colony and on the mainland, pointing out that there were missionaries in many places who were not members of the Church of England. De Cosmos uncharacteristically restrained his own comments, restricting himself to the pithy point that the bishop was "exceedingly artful" in his response.

De Cosmos again took issue with the Church of England early in 1861 when he reprinted a report from a missionary society meeting in London that sympathized with Hills and his difficulties, and pondering: "But for the exertions of the Bishop of Columbia . . . how much of evil would now have been rampant in that distant dependency?" The meeting included the Lord Mayor of London and raised six hundred pounds for the colony. The editor of the *Colonist* was incensed; De Cosmos wrote that Victoria was not the primitive place it was painted to be, "they make out that there are no English here, except those who have not yet lost the scent of the primrose," a pointed dig at the bishop.[4]

*   *   *

The Reverend Cridge and his congregation, because of their prominence in the community, found it difficult to stay out of De Cosmos's newspaper, although the tone of the reporting was not always hostile. The next occasion was much less contentious: a Sunday morning fire in the church, forcing the members to beat a hasty retreat. The fire was caused by an overheated stovepipe, a common occurrence in the wooden buildings of early Victoria. When the fire bell rang, the firemen had a difficult time pulling their equipment through muddy streets. Fortunately, before they arrived the flames were doused by the congregation. Sunday morning worshippers and neighbours successfully tackled the blaze with a bucket brigade and borrowed ladders, but it was a bad omen of things to come. Afterwards the *Colonist* uncharacteristically paid tribute to Douglas, who had been at the service, stating that he had taken over and directed operations with "characteristic coolness."[5]

Hills often appeared to have difficulty striking the right balance in what he said about the colony. A second, much more carefully worded report that he sent to London was again reprinted in Victoria, copied from English papers. Here the bishop told of his travels to the interior goldfields and repeated his hope that some of the many Chinese miners would become Christians and spread the word in "their dark homes in Asia." He continued erroneously to assume they would all return to China. For the second time the bishop stressed the need for middle- and upper-class young women to come to Victoria. But then he went on to add: "where English parents desire for their children English habits, feeling, refinement, and, above all, the pure and sober and evangelical religion of England's Church."[6]

In all this, Hills assumed that most people in the colony were members of the Church of England and of the same mind. But this was not the case as he discovered when E. E. (Ebenezer) Evans, superintendent of the Wesleyan mission for Vancouver Island and the mainland, took him to task for misrepresenting denominational representation in the colony. In response, Hills again went on the offensive, emphasizing that he had seventeen clergy on the Island and the mainland. The Reverend Cridge must have cringed as he saw all his efforts to establish good relations with other faiths damaged by the bishop's haughty tone. De Cosmos drove home the point that other churches were doing more than the Church of England when he reported on the work of Catholic missionaries in the Cowichan area, which had produced a significant drop in drinking and violence.[7]

Hills put up a new gate on his property that obstructed Catholic access to the cemetery. In reality it was a small issue that could have been resolved easily, but Hills was a stubborn man and wanted things his own way. On his side, Demers remained adamant that he wanted easier access. Once again, the Reverend Cridge found himself in the middle of the dispute when he was told to send a key for the gate to Demers. The Roman Catholic primate said this was not good enough because a horse-drawn hearse still could not get through the gate, so any coffin had to be carried manually across Bishop Hills' property. With no reconciliation in sight, Demers took the issue to trial.

The resulting court action found in Demers' favour, and Hills was forced to broaden the gate, providing easy access for all. With much of the community now convinced of Hills' hostile attitude towards other religions, Demers again wrote a letter to the *Colonist* refuting the charges Hills had made against him earlier. He suggested that the newcomer Hills was jealous of Demers' well-established position. With a touch of sarcasm he said he was glad to see that Hills at least recognized what the Catholics had contributed to education. It was another embarrassment for the new bishop and a blow to his standing. Wisely he declined any further comment.

13

Departures and Arrivals

Meanwhile, services at Christ Church took on a new tone with the gift of a bell, rung for the first time on Good Friday 1861. The bell was donated in honour of the bishop by a wealthy Englishwoman, a friend of Miss Burdett-Coutts. It was inscribed: "Glory to God on High; the gift of Hannah Brown for the first church, Right Rev. George Hills, DD, Bishop of Columbia." The ringing of the bell each Sunday morning became a familiar sound in the city of Victoria, a welcome for worshippers as they walked to Christ Church.

But there was trouble looming on the horizon. Rumours from the United States indicated that a civil war was imminent. Victoria was a city with a large American population, and although some supported the Confederate cause, the majority — most of whom were committed to life in Canada — favoured the North. Many had done well financially on

Vancouver Island and contributed financially to the Union. The Wells Fargo manager in Victoria said his company alone had shipped three-hundred-thousand dollars worth of the five-hundred thousand in gold aboard the steamer *Pacific* that had recently left for San Francisco, carrying two hundred miners.

The possibility of civil war to the south was only one of the issues on the minds of these early residents of Victoria. Sickness sometimes plagued the community, and an outbreak of smallpox early in 1862 brought apprehension to everyone in Victoria. The smallpox epidemic struck hardest in the Native camps, and there were reports of hundreds dying. Since the time when Edward and Mary had arrived, other Natives besides the Songhees had set up camps around Victoria. When smallpox came, many of them hurriedly packed their belongings into canoes and left for fishing grounds in the San Juan Islands. Victoria's small police force was ordered to stop more Natives from coming into town so they would not contract the disease and spread it further, and several groups from northern bands who had moved south to be near the colony were told to return home. As fear of the disease grew, everyone was on edge and the gunboat HMS *Grappler* moved into the harbour to maintain the peace.

The Haida camp became badly infected, and its inhabitants, often the most severely affected by this disease, were ordered to go home. Three hundred of them left for the Queen Charlotte Islands. The *Colonist* reported: "The poor creatures protested feelingly against the justice of the proceeding, but manifested no desire to resist the stern mandate of the law.... The gunboat, at the urgent request of the chief, will accompany and protect the Indians until they have passed Nanaimo — the Indians of which place have many old scores to wipe out in consequence of outrages received at the hands of the [Haida] in years gone by."[1] After their departure, authorities found a number of bodies at the abandoned camp at Ogden Point. The Reverend Cridge mentioned the suffering Natives many times in his Sunday sermons and offered prayers for their survival and safe return to their homes.

Since the arrival of Bishop Hills, a number of ministers had been persuaded to come to Vancouver Island. In the absence of medical professionals, ministers took up the case of trying to aid the sick. The Reverend A. C. Garrett was working in a makeshift hospital on the Songhees reserve, where the initial death toll was twenty. Two other Anglican clergy were reported ready to travel north to treat the sick, leading the *Colonist* to observe, perhaps unfairly, "We are happy to perceive that the clergy are moving in the matter at last. 'Better late than never.'"[2] The handling of the smallpox epidemic has been much discussed in recent times, some analysts arguing that sending the Native peoples back to their homes up the coast only helped to spread the disease. In Victoria itself, the disease was held in check to a degree with quarantine procedures.

After the epidemic had run its course, Cridge was able to return to his regular duties. There was to be a new organ for the church, but he happily turned the problem over to a committee. His work as school superintendant took up much of his time in visits to the individual schools in Victoria and beyond. On one occasion he even received support in this area from the *Colonist*, which lambasted the government for its lack of funding for public education despite the increase in the number of children. It praised Cridge for his "ability and zeal" but added that one man could only do so much.[3]

Happily married himself, and with the evidence all around him of the positive influence of women on the men of Victoria, the Reverend Cridge was among those anxious to have more women move to the colony. He advocated that older orphans and women down on their luck in England should be encouraged to come to Victoria to work as domestics until such time as they could marry and have children. It was a long wait, but in September 1862 there was great excitement among the colony's many bachelors when a ship sponsored by the Church of England, the *Tynemouth*, docked. The women had been carefully selected from the ranks of English congregations. One had died en route, leaving sixty-two still aboard. A *Colonist* writer boarded the ship to have a good look at the women, and wrote,

"They are mostly cleanly, well-built, pretty looking young women — varying from fourteen to an uncertain figure." He added ungallantly, "A few are young widows who have seen better days." He found that "most appear to have been well raised and generally they seem a superior lot to the women usually met with on emigrant vessels." Men who tried to get aboard were thrown off, and there had been some "trouble" with the crew on the crossing, a reference to incidents similar to the one on the Cridges' long voyage.[4]

Cridge was pleased to learn that some thirty of these women were hired as domestic servants even before disembarking. There was certainly great interest in the women's arrival, for the *Colonist* reported: "A large and anxious crowd of breeches-wearing bipeds assembled to see the women disembark, and generally expressed themselves well pleased with their appearance."[5] The ribald remarks and laughter of the men caused Cridge to cringe, for he abhorred foul language. The paper ran a humorous comment regarding the women, saying two ministers — no names given but one was Cridge — and a military officer were seen patrolling the fence enclosing the building where the women were housed. This followed an instance when a woman had been seen talking to a man through the wire enclosure. The two vigilant clergymen felt it their duty to act as protectors of the women's virtue, said the writer, who then wryly suggested that marines be ordered "to bayonet every young man who may have the audacity to approach within speaking distance of the women."[6]

To mark the arrival of the women, the Reverend Cridge led a special service at Christ Church. The sermon was given by the Reverend M. Scott, who had accompanied them on the trip. He asked the women to remember their religious duties and always to shape their conduct so as to be a credit to their English mothers. The remark was far from helpful, for many of the women were already homesick. The Reverend Scott went on to advise them that "when beset by sin and temptation to rely on a kind Providence for aid and comfort."[7] The *Colonist* reported that there was hardly a dry eye in Christ Church when he finished.

Years later, it was admitted that many of the women were not prepared to keep house and marry lusty miners, and some departed quickly for work in what passed at the time for Victoria's bright lights. The *Victoria Directory* listed seven hotels and restaurants and six saloons in Victoria, including the Star and Garter, Music Hall and Phoenix, where some of the women may have found employment. One advertisement called for two girls to be barmaids at the Victoria Lager Beer Saloon at Johnson and Store streets, stressing they had to be respectable.

The Reverend Cridge was somewhat disappointed with the reception given some of the *Tynemouth* women. "There were often cruel remarks from the pompous class," commented the Victoria baker Samuel Nesbitt, referring to comments he had overheard about his own "boat bride," Jane.[8] Victoria was taking on many of the aspects of a small city, with its attendant larger problems and frustrations, and although he could not deal with everything, Cridge was in the midst of it all.

14

Victoria — A City of Almost Six Thousand

The Reverend Cridge was the only Protestant clergyman until 1858, and although he was soon joined by other pastors arriving in increasing numbers to minister to Methodists, Wesleyans, Congregationalists and Presbyterians, because he was there first he was more involved with the development of the community itself than any of the others.

The problems associated with the growth of the community multiplied, requiring more official oversight. Victoria's first city council meeting was held in August 1862, a year after Douglas's decree made it a city. One of the council's first dictates was to introduce regulations ordering that traffic keep to the left side of the road or face a five-pound fine. At the same time, Christian religious leaders hailed an amendment made by the council to the legislature's Sunday closing law. It called for a twenty-pound fine for anyone over fourteen engaged in buying or selling any kind of labour on Sunday unless it was absolutely necessary or for charitable purposes. The exceptions were bakers and butchers, who needed to work on Sunday to open for business on Monday. Some business owners were unhappy with the new rule, and council expected trouble over interpretation of the word "necessary."

With so much of pioneer life centred on the Church, many families observed what were called "Silent Sundays," a day reserved strictly for prayers and for attending church services. Two local men, George Lay and J. L. Langley, presented a fourteen-name petition to the city council calling on them to enforce the so-called "blue laws" requiring the observance of the Sabbath. To the dismay of some, the colonial authorities acted on the petition, and shutters went up on stores and places of entertainment on Sundays. Blinds had always been drawn on the homes of the faithful, and there was little activity except for church services on Sundays, but now all businesses, like it or not, had to close.

Sunday practices in most Christian homes were strict. Meals were prepared the night before, and dirty dishes waited until Monday to be washed. Children's books, other than those dealing with religious topics, and toys were put away in drawers and cupboards. For children in particular, restrictions were severe and tedious. They always dressed in their best clothes on Sunday, were not allowed to shout or make a noise, and could not run or play games outside. Walking was the only activity permitted apart from religious observances.

Not always staid and sedate, the people of Victoria often made up for silent Sundays by their behaviour on other days of the week. In November 1862, the city marked the birthday of the Prince of Wales. Celebrations began with an early morning ear-splitting canon salute, followed by special events and horse races at the recently completed track. An evening dinner at the Lyceum Hall featured many toasts and patriotic songs, including "Rule Britannia" and even "The Roast Beef of Old England."

England was far from the scene but always in the hearts of the early Victorians, as evidenced by a crowd of some three hundred that gathered in early 1863 to discuss the Lancashire Relief Fund. The Reverend Cridge had taken an active role in this relief effort, although it was an ecumenical drive organized by all the local churches aimed to relieve some of the poverty and starvation prevalent in northern England because of the American Civil War. Union ships were blockading Southern ports, preventing the export of cotton to the mills of Lancashire. Many English mills had been forced to close, and thousands were out of work, barely surviving in wretched poverty. Bishop Hills proposed a resolution sympathizing with the people's plight and praising them for their patience and fortitude. The Reverend Cridge headed a committee to canvas the James Bay district for funds, while Bishop Demers led a group that looked after the Fort Street area. The target was four thousand dollars but the final total raised was more than five thousand, which the *Colonist* noted was good for such a small community.[1]

The city continued to expand. The firm of Howard and Barnett produced the first comprehensive local directory for 1863, although there had been a partial one two years earlier. It stated that there were fifteen hundred buildings, "which seems very creditable for the size of the city."[2] There were three commodious brick hotels: the St. Nicholas, the St. George and the Royal; five churches: two Church of England and one each Catholic, Wesleyan and Congregational, as well as a Presbyterian church and a Jewish synagogue under construction. The Jewish community had recently conducted a fundraising drive to erect a brick building. Construction had also begun on a four-mile-long railway to Esquimalt, and the water supply now came from Elk Lake, eight miles away. The directory reported that exports were booming, although the fishery was neglected. It also noted that agriculture was on the upswing, with immigrants snapping up land costing four shillings two pence per acre. In keeping with the times, the directory recognized only male members of the community. Edward Cridge was listed but not his wife, Mary, his sisters or any other females in Victoria. By this time Edward and Mary had been living in Victoria for eight years.

With church affairs in good order and no crises on the horizon, Bishop

Hills left in April 1863 for England, where he would make a personal report after three years in his new diocese and raise new funds to continue the work of the church. The *Colonist* forgot for the moment its past hostility towards the bishop and said that the clergyman had a favourable effect on the "social, moral, material, and religious elevation of the inhabitants of his diocese."[3]

Bishop Demers had just returned from a trip to the Cowichan Valley and was credited with persuading the Natives there to surrender three of their members wanted for killing two white men. The esteem and respect in which he was held by the Natives was responsible for the peaceful resolution of this offence.[4] The Natives arrested were tried, found guilty and hanged, very much in frontier style.

Life took another turn for De Cosmos when he finally won a Victoria-area seat in the legislative assembly in 1863. He immediately announced that after five years of ownership he was selling the paper to devote himself full-time to politics. The *Colonist* was bought by five of his employees, and although the old tormenter was gone, his style remained: the new owners continued to attack the Hudson's Bay Company, the government and other factions that raised their ire. Although he had been a successful publisher, De Cosmos was less than an inspiring politician. He was, however, consistent, and he worked tirelessly for two causes: the joining of Vancouver Island and the mainland and the establishment of a new province within Canadian confederation.

Cridge occasionally ran afoul of the new *Colonist* ownership. For instance, he was sharply criticized for refusing to give Christian burial to a youth named Sheppard who died following a liquor-induced disturbance in a public bar. Cridge said he had his reasons but declined to name them, and so another minister conducted the burial. The man had been a sailor aboard HMS *Forward*. Cridge despised drunkenness and the adverse effects of liquor, especially on the Native population. Throughout his life he preached against the evils of liquor. It is believed that alcohol was the source of his own father's financial problems and possibly also his death.[5]

Bishop Hills continued to be a strong booster of the Crown colony of British Columbia in the United Kingdom. He told one audience of the colony's abundance of resources, citing the case of a young girl who went fishing for herring with a rake and very quickly filled a bucket. With Hills away in England, the Reverend Cridge travelled to various other communities that were not normally his responsibility, raising funds for the British and Foreign Bible Society.[6] Although busy with her growing family and community interests, Mary Cridge found time to add a wistful comment to a short letter she sent to her husband while he was on the road. She began, "To my own dearest husband." She assured him that the family was getting on well. However, she added, "There is one who is somewhat lonely without the one of her heart." She signed the letter, "Your fond wife, Mary Cridge."[7]

*　*　*

As part of his duties as a religious leader in the community, the Reverend Cridge presided at a Victoria meeting in 1863 when a large audience turned out to hear the outspoken, radical missionary William Duncan, who was high charismatic but dangerously authoritarian.[8] If eccentricity was common among this breed of men, Duncan stood out spectacularly. He had been asked to leave a Church of England missionary training school for reasons not made public and arrived in Victoria in 1857 with his own mission clear in his mind. The young Englishman headed immediately to Fort Simpson, five hundred miles north of Victoria, now the city of Prince Rupert. He was warned that it was dangerous country and that he stood the chance of being slain by hostile Tsimshians if he ventured outside the fort.

Danger did not daunt Duncan, for he was determined to set up a model community in the hinterland, adhering to his own ideals. He favoured complete assimilation of Natives and whites. One of his first goals, however, was to keep the Natives away from "depraved and demoralizing whites."[9] He founded the small Native community of Metlakatla, some seventeen miles south of Fort Simpson, as his utopian Christian village.

Several years had passed since he had begun his assimilation project, and he was visiting Victoria to raise more funds. Cridge in his introduction to the meeting reminded the audience that it was the responsibility of the clergy to spread the gospel, adding that Christianity should take precedence over civilization. The flamboyant Duncan was the antithesis of the quiet Cridge, but the two men seemed to get along, possibly because they shared a mistrust of clerical hierarchy. They were both opposed to alcohol, and both had seen the problems alcohol created among the Native people. Cridge invited the missionary to stay at his home on his visits to Victoria.

Duncan had the audience gasping as he told of wresting power from medicine men and witnessing "scenes of horror" where he claimed Natives ate human flesh. It is clear that he had no idea of the role of shamans in native spirituality, but he played on the settlers' misconceptions. He explained that he sought to convert Natives to an English way of life and culture, right down to speaking the language, wearing the clothes and living in English-style homes. Despite some resistance, he had established a prosperous community based on fishing and the utilization of other local resources. Duncan claimed to have eliminated face painting, the tearing up of property of the deceased, gambling, and several other Native practices. He said there were now thirty-seven English-style homes built in Metlakatla as well as a large church.

Duncan's goal, as he explained to the meeting, was to keep liquor out and to keep the Natives in the community, where they would be safe from the evils brought by the Europeans. In this attempt he was remarkably successful in the beginning. But there was another side to Duncan, and he enforced his rigid rules with the help of some heavy-handed Native police he had trained. What began as an intriguing experiment for the Church of England, visited by Bishop Hills in its early stages, eventually deteriorated under Duncan's eccentric control, leading to a clash with the Church of England in 1881. Duncan and some three hundred and fifty followers eventually left Metlakatla for Alaska, where he established New Metlakatla in 1887.

15

Douglas Retires from Office

The retirement of James Douglas, the father of the colony, in 1864 marked the end of an era. It was an emotional time for the Cridge family. Douglas's departure dramatically underscored the power he and the Hudson's Bay Company had held since the trader began working for them in 1822. Now he was the retiring governor, the grand old man moving on. Even his sharpest critics, including the *Colonist*, had nothing but nice things to say.

Douglas was credited with staving off the threat of American domination. His steady but tough hand had ensured law and order was kept in the goldfields when trouble loomed. Victoria was now a well-established community with a growing population; settlements were being founded throughout the Island and on the mainland. The colony had an elected governing assembly, and its economy was booming, with lumber exports shipped as far as Australia. The settlement had grown in less than ten years from a population of some three hundred when the Cridges arrived to more than six thousand.

The British colonial office stated in tribute to the retiring governor: "Sir James Douglas's career as governor has been a remarkable one. He now quits his two Govts. [Vancouver Island and B.C.] leaving them in a state of prosperity, with every prospect of greater advancement."[1] A committee of leading citizens organized a farewell dinner that was held a few days before his departure for Britain, on May 14, 1864. It was a "glorious and brilliant evening," according to the *Colonist*. With military men in uniform displaying their medals and everyone else decked out in their best, the ground floor of the Victoria Theatre, its walls draped with Union Jacks, was a colourful scene that evening. The dinner was Victoria's social event of the year, albeit largely a male affair. Ladies attired in their finest could watch the proceedings from the theatre's upper boxes and dress circle. Glasses were raised in many toasts to the founding father, and a band blared out "There's a Good Time Coming," which was presumably no reflection on the governor's rule. Douglas's short speech received a "tremendous cheer" when he said that there had been magnificent achievements and that the colony's progress "was on the right course."[2]

The Cridges were in the large, waving crowd at the waterfront a few days later as Douglas and his family rode through flag-bedecked streets to board the ship that would take them on a year-long visit to England, courtesy of the British government. A band played "For He's a Jolly Good Fellow" and "Auld Lang Syne" as the ship moved away from the pier to the thunder of a booming salute by naval guns.

The new governor was Captain Arthur Edward Kennedy, who had held the same post in Western Australia and was given much credit for the development of the city of Perth. Kennedy was officially welcomed by Douglas just prior to his departure and by the town's many factions, including the Chinese residents, who informed him there were now about two thousand of them in the two colonies: some three to four hundred in Victoria and most of the remainder in the interior goldfields. They expressed loyalty and respect for the law and emphasized the importance of trade.

Kennedy was a no-nonsense governor who had little experience dealing with or listening to elected officials. As a result, many clashes occurred during his relatively brief tenure. He announced that he intended to make major changes in education, and he did not hesitate to voice his views on the subject when the Reverend Cridge led a delegation representing the Church of England, in the absence of Bishop Hills, to welcome him to Vancouver Island. Entering the meeting with some apprehension, Cridge attempted to strike the right tone by pledging the group's loyalty. He explained with some pride that the Church of England now had eight ministers in and around Victoria, some of them with teaching duties, and he stressed that they received no government money.

In a peremptory fashion, Kennedy asked if it had ever occurred to them that it would lower costs if there were fewer and more efficient schools. The new governor than stated he wanted a completely non-sectarian system, stressing that he had seen the evil results of boys educated to denounce the religion of others, perhaps a reference to what he had heard about Bishop Hills' comments some years earlier. Kennedy stated that churches could continue to teach religion in Sunday schools, but general education must be non-sectarian. The Reverend Cridge and the other ministers left the meeting in disarray, dismayed with the shape of things to come. The *Colonist*, however, praised the new governor's policy: "We are fortunate in getting a Governor whose ideas on this important question are unclogged by the antiquated prejudices of well-meaning but mistaken clergymen."[3] Many parents agreed wholeheartedly.

A subsequent report prepared by the education committee of the legislative assembly supported Kennedy's position. It found that there was no statute governing education and noted that the colony had leaned heavily on Reverend Cridge, still unpaid, for assistance. The committee found that the system was now totally inadequate and called for public funds for the creation of non-sectarian schools and the appointment of a full-time superintendent of education. Three hundred people signed a petition backing a common, non-religious school system, and five hundred residents packed the Victoria Theatre for a meeting chaired by Mayor Thomas Harris. At this meeting, J. J. Cochrane, who stressed he was a member of the Church of England, proposed a resolution calling for free common schools that would be non-sectarian, efficient and open to all.[4]

Aware that he held a losing point of view, the Reverend Charles Wood, principal of a Church of England school, agreed that schools should be open to all. He contended that the present system could be non-sectarian while still recommending the Bible as the foundation of true education. A voice from the balcony demanded, "What Bible?" Wood did not answer. The Reverend Cridge backed his colleague Wood, and argued that the total elimination of religious teaching would be disastrous. There were many supporting cries of "hear, hear." Cridge was applauded when he said his definition of tolerance was that people should not impose their ideas on others. But he was challenged from the audience and asked if he favoured no education at all if it was not religious. Cridge picked his words carefully, saying he thought that children could be properly educated without religious instruction, but he was firmly convinced that religious education was not impossible in the colony.

The vote, nevertheless, was loud in support of the resolution for non-sectarian schools. When Wood challenged the vote, Harris told him to turn around and look at the audience, and then called the vote again. There was another loud cheer and a reporter said he saw a "forest of arms" raised in support. Within weeks the assembly passed a bill legalizing public schools. It faced continued opposition from some religious leaders, however, and a prolonged debate about money before free, non-sectarian education was entrenched and functioning. Establishing public schools was a long, drawn-out process, and not until 1872 did a non-sectarian education system finally became law.

The Reverend Cridge had been entrusted with the education of the Island's children from 1856, and he had devoted much of his time to ensuring it was the best that could be provided. His term as superintendent of education ended in 1865, when he was finally relieved of his duties. He would miss his involvement with the children. The government appointed Alfred Waddington to replace him, but Waddington left the position as school superintendent after only one year in order to build a wagon road from Bute Inlet to the interior goldfields. Engineers had already looked at the area and said it was too rugged for such a road, but Waddington was determined to try. Not too long after he began the project, racial tension boiled over, and word reached Victoria of a massacre near Bute Inlet in a clash between workers and Natives. A handful of survivors told of Natives firing into their tents as people slept. Some nineteen men died.

The prospects of an all-out racial war loomed, and Cridge recalled the earlier deaths of miners on the Fraser when the Native people attempted to stop the gold rush. As soon as the news of Bute Inlet reached Victoria, vigilantes called for guns and ammunition to be transported to the scene so that the killers could be hunted down. The *Colonist* suggested the new Victoria Volunteer Rifle Corps be sent, but not in their new fancy uniforms for fear they would easily be "picked off by the skulking savages."[5] Cridge attempted to calm the antagonism towards the Natives. Sadly though, the killings even inflamed Cridge's colleague the Reverend Garrett, who had tended Natives on the Songhees reserve during the smallpox epidemic. Garrett stated angrily that he had changed his views about Natives; he now believed that they should be treated "with truth, justice and severity." Garrett said white men could not look on calmly while "our brethren had their hearts torn from their bodies."[6] For Cridge it was a sad reversal for a man he had come to admire.

Drawing on his years of experience in Australia, Governor Kennedy did not respond to demands for a major military movement to Bute Inlet or for vigilante action. Instead, he assumed Cridge's more measured response and called in local Natives to discuss the situation. As a result, there was no volunteer posse roaming the hinterland, anger died down, and Natives cooperated in bringing the killers to justice. Several were arrested, and five were tried and hanged for the crime. The *Colonist* reported that "the wretched creatures evinced no fear of death and died with scarce a struggle."[7]

Although Waddington's route to the interior was doomed to fail, much later he received a tribute for his pioneering zeal and enthusiasm when British Columbia's highest peak, at the head of Bute Inlet, was named after him. Only recently have people begun to realize that the Natives at Bute Inlet might have had reason to be angry at Waddington's intrusion into their lands.

16

Tragedy at Home

As Edward Cridge strove to look after the souls of his congregation, the reputation of his church and the welfare of his community, Mary continued to care for her growing brood of children and to support her husband's and her own causes. Conditions at the parsonage were very different in 1864 than they had been in 1856, when they first moved in. There were now six Cridge children: Richard, the eldest; Edward, born in 1857; Mary; the twins Grace and Eber; and baby Frederick, the fourth son. Their mother Mary and her sister-in-law Elizabeth had become firm friends, and the two often worked side by side on projects at home as well as on forays into the community to aid the sick and the needy. With his many children and all their noise, Edward often rose early to prepare his sermons. The parsonage was a happy, bustling place, and the Cridge family was looking forward to a joyous Christmas that year. They had a healthy family around them, and Edward had been elevated from rector to dean of Christ Church in recognition of his many services to the Church and the colony. The family's joy, however, soon turned to unimagined sorrow.

Dean Cridge became busier than usual in November as he consoled sorrowing parents of numerous children in the colony who were dying from a virulent strain of black measles. Decades before the discovery of sulpha drugs and antibiotics, infectious diseases often took a deadly toll among the young, the old and the frail. Edward and Mary came to know well that toll as they shared the grief that wracked their congregation. They prayed daily for the sick children, but just three weeks before Christmas, the epidemic suddenly worsened, striking more and more of the young and the helpless. As the disease swept from one house to the next, and then from one child to the next, inevitably it arrived at the parsonage and struck first the new baby, Frederick, who was only ten months old. It claimed his life on December 11. Despite all the efforts of their parents and Dr. Helmcken, the other Cridge children also became infected, and so began the saddest days of their lives for Edward and Mary.

Seven-year-old Edward suffered terribly. Mary and her sister-in-law Elizabeth spent most of their days and nights at his bedside, trying to help him as he struggled for breath and burned up with fever. The disease then spread to twins Grace and Eber, and every adult in the household took their turn tending the sick children. Their efforts were to no avail. Edward died on February 4, 1865, and within ten days the twins also lay still and lifeless. Grace and Eber had been approaching their third birthday when they died. Edward and Mary feared that all their children could be taken from them and prayed to God for compassion.

Finally spring brought with it warmer days, the arrival of the first flowers in the garden, and at last the abatement of the epidemic. Only two of the Cridge children, Richard, now aged nine, and Mary, aged five, survived. As the grief-stricken couple began to look to the future, they took some small consolation when Mary found that once again she was pregnant.

Edgar Fawcett, who knew the Cridges for more than fifty years and was at one time tutored by the minister, wrote about their tragedy. The article appeared in the *Colonist* in 1913. Fawcett described Cridge in his later years as a "dear old man," whom he had watched in a time of great sorrow during the deaths of his children. Fawcett described the funeral processions for which Cridge was the principal mourner: "This scene was on the occasion of the burial of one of his children and it was repeated three times in as many weeks as the angel of death entered the rectory four times taking one olive branch after another through black measles, the little white coffins being carried to the cemetery."[1]

Fawcett noted the inscriptions on the tombstone in Victoria's first cemetery, located just north of Christ Church. To this day, chiselled on its face are words that provide stark evidence of the sorrows of pioneer life: "Frederick Pemberton, died December 11, 1864, Aged 10 months; Edward Scott, died February 4, 1865, Aged 7 years, 8 months; Eber, died February 11, 1865, Aged 2 years, 10 months; Grace, died February 13, 1865, Aged 2 years, 10 months; children of Edward and Mary Cridge."

The Christ Church congregation tearfully expressed their sympathy. None shared their sorrow more than John Muir, the mill owner from Sooke. Muir wrote, "Our most respected friend was called to mark the loss, not only of many of his loyal parishioners but also four of his own children. He had always shown himself to be the gentlest of men, and certainly his faith continued to lie firmly in the hands of his Lord and Master, but it was difficult for him not to question the divine reasoning behind such a burden."[2]

The dean refused to excuse himself from any duties and carried on despite the terrible loss. Mary found the parsonage frighteningly quiet. Their sorrow was beyond understanding, but together as time elapsed they found some solace in each other and in their faith. Living in the parsonage with constant reminders of the children they had lost, however, became unbearable, and Edward took the opportunity in April to purchase Sellindge Cottage from Captain McNeil for $814.

The house was located well away from the town in the relatively undeveloped area of Oak Bay, across Beach Drive from the present Oak Bay Marina. Cridge kept detailed accounts of his finances, including the cost of having the chimney cleaned and the walls whitewashed prior to moving in. A diary entry states how happy they were to be moving away from the parsonage into a house that they could really call their own, not provided by the colony or the Church. It was not the home the dean had envisioned — that would wait until later — but Sellindge was their own, a cottage they could furnish as they wished and which provided a refuge in difficult times.

Mary faced her seventh pregnancy with some trepidation. It was emotionally a difficult time for her, and when Rhoda was born July 13, 1865, Mary's worst fears were realized when the new baby became terribly ill. Dr. Helmcken was called and he rushed to Sellindge Cottage. It seemed the end was near for tiny Rhoda, and her father wrote in his diary that she looked like death, something with which he had become all too familiar. Days later Rhoda still clung to life, and finally he was able to confirm, "She looked to us as one who was raised from the dead." Rhoda unfortunately suffered ill health for much of her life and died in 1886 at age twenty-one.

Two more daughters were born at the cottage: Ellen on March 18, 1867, and Maude on August 20, 1868. Maude was Edward and Mary's ninth and last child. She was their fifth daughter, destined to be a spinster who would care for other members of the family and her parents in their old age. Edward and Mary at this time had five living children. Only three would outlive them: Mary, Ellen, and Maude.

The Cridges knew that the cottage would not adequately fill their needs in the long term, and Edward held tightly to his dream of building Marifield. The land he owned was part of what was originally the Beckley Farm estate in James Bay, three acres situated on the west side of Government Street, bordered by what are now Toronto and Simcoe streets. His down payment on the fourteen-hundred-dollar property in 1860 had been nine hundred dollars. Until new funds could be found, the home remained a dream.

Richard, the Cridges' oldest child, was the only son who survived the

The Misses Cridge, Maude, Ellen and Mary, daughters
of Edward and Mary Cridge, c. 1870
(BC ARCHIVES, A-01209 / PHOTO: STEPHEN ALLEN SPENCER)

epidemic. He soon left the family fold and travelled to England to further his education. Edward paid a hundred and thirty dollars for Richard's passage when he left in 1870 at the age of fourteen. The young man boarded a ship in Victoria that travelled down the Pacific coast to Panama, retracing the same route Bishop Hills had taken, across the isthmus by train to the Atlantic before the long voyage by ship to England. Richard's studies in England led to his qualifying as a civil engineer. He returned to Victoria and then travelled the world as an engineer. He died in 1906 in Hawaii.

17

Political Changes and
a Suspicious Fire

A fter a year's absence, Bishop Hills returned from England in the
spring of 1864 and gave residents something new to talk about. He
brought with him a wife, the former Miss Maria Philadelphia Louisa King,
born in 1823, the daughter of an English admiral. She was well versed in
the duties of a bishop's spouse and accompanied him to functions, snipped
ribbons, and distributed prizes at school events. To the local Church of
England community she was the bishop's wife, a figure to be respected,
but she never truly mixed freely with the church congregation as Mary
Cridge had done. Although it was said the bishop listened carefully to her
advice, Mrs. Hills was not demonstrative in public, remaining quietly in
the background at her husband's side, observing rather than participating.

Dean Cridge was delighted when, with the support of Bishop Hills, he finally saw one of his recommendations coming to fruition in a major step forward in education. He was present at the laying of the cornerstone for the Collegiate School for Girls, the Anglicans' answer to Bishop Demers' St. Ann's School. Governor Kennedy was there and poured some oil on troubled waters by stating he was glad to see people reconciling their differences and meeting the increasing educational needs of the growing community. The governor said he was sure the school would produce girls who were "good and virtuous mothers."[1] He was also convinced that the school would not advocate a narrow or sectarian approach to life. Bishop Hills carefully stressed in his own remarks that England had a deep interest in its colonies and their Christian development. In its report of the ceremony, the *Colonist* did not indicate whether or not Bishop Demers was among the many clergy present.

The completion of the telegraph line to Victoria on July 30, 1866, gave the city a new link to the outside world. Flags fluttered all over town on this momentous occasion; banks and stores closed and the mayor declared a public half-holiday. Ships' guns roared a salute at six o'clock in the evening, and an hour later crowds started to gather on Government Street. The volunteers' militia band led a parade of about fifteen hundred to the assembly buildings, which were located on the site of today's parliament buildings and were often referred to as "the birdcages." There a great cheer went up when it was learned that the first wire had been received. Governor Kennedy made a brief speech and stated that this occasion was the happiest moment of his time in the colony. There were three cheers for Queen Victoria and another three for the U.S. president.

The parade, led by firemen with burning torches, marched downtown, where a huge bonfire was ignited and fireworks soon lit up the night sky. Church bell-ringers joined in the celebrations. The *Colonist* waxed quite lyrical in its report: "The merry sound of the bells yesterday morning, as they pealed forth a tribute of praise to the genius of the scientific minds of the age, announced the glad tidings that the Old World has been united with the New."[2]

The next day, July 31, Mayor Lumley Franklin asked the residents to contribute to the cost of sending a wire of congratulations to London. When it was found that the cost would be a hefty hundred and fifty dollars, about ten dollars per word, the hat had to go around again to raise more funds. The wire addressed to the Lord Mayor of London stated: "The infant colony of Vancouver Island eight thousand miles distant sends cordial greetings to Mother England." It was signed "Lumley Franklin, Mayor." After the arrival of telegraph service, there were other signs that the outside world was coming closer. The local businessman Harry Pickett left for Adelaide, Australia, to open a colonial agency for Burrard Inlet Lumber as the demand for timber and spars grew.

The colonial governor and the legislative assembly seemed to be more frequently at loggerheads with Amor De Cosmos now that he was an elected member. Never one to resist an argument, he claimed that there was illegal interference from the governor in the allocation and spending of public funds. He also kept the heat on another of his favourite topics, the union of the two colonies: Vancouver Island and the mainland. At this time the larger topic of Canadian Confederation was also on the horizon, and the two issues were often conjoined. At a Young Men's Institute meeting in 1865, the vote following a freewheeling debate of whether to join with the United States or Canada was eight for the United States and republicanism and thirty-seven for the monarchy. The count underlined the majority opinion of the residents on Vancouver Island.

Amalgamation of the two colonies came in August 1866 with the British parliament passing an Act of Union. There was, however, little excitement at noon on November 19, 1866, when the union was proclaimed simultaneously in Victoria and New Westminster. Governor Kennedy had taken the brunt of the arguments for and against in his role as governor. His tenure came to an end, much to his own satisfaction, after two years of constant battle with the assembly. Frederick Seymour, governor of the mainland colony, became the first governor of the united colony of British Columbia. It took another two years of debate, however, before the site of the capital was decided. Victoria finally emerged as the winner, largely because of its population, and New Westminster subsequently suffered an economic slowdown, much to the chagrin of its residents.

The creation of Canada, which united four eastern provinces on July 1, 1867, raised little excitement in Victoria. It was almost an abstraction, as many were more concerned about British Columbia's difficult position on the Pacific, squeezed between two U.S. territories. The Americans had just purchased Alaska some four months earlier from Russia. Some of the strong U.S. contingent in Victoria still predicted the entire Pacific coast would soon become a part of the United States.

Dean Cridge gave little evidence of his feelings on these matters that shaped the future for the community, and there is nothing in his diaries about regional politics. Instead, he and his church colleagues stayed away from the debate. Edward and Mary watched as their world in Victoria changed, and tried to guide their congregation as the Church had taught them.

As often seemed to be the case, happiness was tempered with sadness for Mary and Edward. Dean Cridge was not an overly emotional man. He had learned to provide sympathy to others in times of need without sad events outwardly affecting him, but his usually impassive face showed evident sorrow on the morning of October 2, 1869, as he looked at the smoking wreckage of his beloved Christ Church. He had been instrumental in its construction, he had named it after the church where he had been ordained in England, and for nearly thirteen years he had proudly taken his place in its pulpit and preached the gospel to an ever growing congregation. Now only charred timbers remained of the community's first church.

Fire had been spotted on the roof at about nine o'clock the previous evening, a Friday. Someone ran to the fire hall, raised the alarm, and the clanging bell could be heard all over town. Yet when the firemen arrived there was really nothing they could do. It was impossible to save the wooden building because the flames already had such a strong hold. All they could do was prevent the blaze from spreading to nearby houses. The dean was not there when the roof fell in and the blaze lit up the night sky, but he stood with tears in his eyes the next morning as he viewed the blackened remains. Nothing was left, and the loss was estimated at about twenty thousand dollars.

Speculation surfaced about the cause; arson was suspected but an investigation found nothing. A choir practice had taken place two days earlier, but no candles or lamps had been lit. The weather for all of September had been warm, and the heating stoves had not been used since April. Dean Cridge solemnly comforted his congregation as they stood around him on the soot-covered church grounds. He told them they now had the challenge of rebuilding a bigger and better Christ Church. His quiet confidence and determination spurred them on. Bishop Hills was responsible for replacing the church, but the congregation looked to Dean Cridge for direction. Christ Church had always been his; he had been its inspiration and driving force from the beginning. Less than two years later a new building stood on the site, a larger wooden structure that would serve the congregation through turbulent times until a stone church was erected many years later.

The coming year was to be a trouble-filled one for the Church of England and the new colony of British Columbia. Governor Frederick Seymour died suddenly in the summer of 1870, and the British colonial office appointed Anthony Musgrave, previously governor of Newfoundland, to the post. He was a personal friend of Sir John A. Macdonald, Canada's first prime minister, and was instructed to push British Columbia to enter Confederation. The British government believed that because of U.S. territorial ambitions and other international developments, its political and economic interests would be best served if British Columbia became part of Canada. Although there were a few exceptions, Cridge's congregation was largely in favour of this move, and Amor De Cosmos had been preaching this for years. In eastern Canada, however, many thought it would be folly to spend money on a tiny far-distant community in the wilderness.

Macdonald saw the bigger picture, and Musgrave pushed the question in the B.C. assembly. There was heated debate but a delegation finally visited Ottawa to negotiate the terms. British Columbia's conditions were agreed to on April 6, 1870. They included elimination of the provincial debt; a per capita grant for 60,000 people, much larger than the actual population; and construction of a transportation link between the East and the West. The colony's population at this time was 8,500 settlers and 25,700 natives. The province was allocated three senators and six Members of Parliament and became part of Canada on July 21, 1871. De Cosmos and the Confederationists were ecstatic, but most adopted a wait-and-see attitude. There was no great public outpouring of feeling. Helmcken, who remained a member of the assembly, declined the invitation to form the first B.C. provincial government, and in the subsequent election a lawyer without previous political experience, John Foster McCreight, became the first premier. Also elected was De Cosmos, who won one of the six seats in Ottawa — it was permissible at this time to be elected to both the provincial and federal houses. The elections might have been over, but there remained some stormy days ahead.

As was to become the rule, British Columbia's political cauldron continued to boil. After little more than a year in office, McCreight was defeated on a non-confidence vote. Picked to succeed him was the fiery old radical and iconoclast himself, Amor De Cosmos. Those who expected fireworks were quickly disappointed. As premier, De Cosmos would discover it was easier to light a spark than to put it out. He found that criticizing the government was much easier than being the person in charge.

18

Mary's Orphanage

As the Christ Church congregation concentrated its energies on the construction of a new church, another worrisome problem surfaced. Numbers of homeless children were appearing on the streets. Fearing for the future of the youngsters, the women of the congregation began offering these orphans food and shelter, looking for any spare bed they could find. When their own homes would take no more, they approached friends and other members of the congregation, but it was clear that the problem was increasing.

The children were mostly youngsters whose mothers had died, some of them in childbirth, others during an epidemic of smallpox or black measles. Some had been left with fathers who then abandoned them or left them with a neighbour when they went off to find gold or to make a living out of town. The children were aged from about six or eight to fourteen.

Mary enlisted the aid of her old friend the senator's wife, Catherine Macdonald, and together they looked for a solution. They recruited the assistance of women from their own congregation and from three other Protestant churches. The shortage of space at Sellindge, and Mary's concern for the orphans, prompted her to recommend to Edward that the family move back to the parsonage. There, she reasoned, there would be more room to take in the hungry waifs on a short-term basis until a more permanent place could be found. The family made the move back late in 1871. Although the family retainer Mary Herbert had married and moved to Langley in the Fraser Valley, Mr. and Mrs. Raby remained and assisted with the move back.

With five children of her own, and still mourning the four who had died, Mary took into her own home at least one orphan, Mary-Anne Bastien, a teenager. Mrs. Macdonald took in others, as did many women in the community. Still the numbers needing help swamped their ability to accommodate them. The women decided an orphanage was the only plausible answer. Dedicated to a new cause, Mary and Catherine asked the Reverend Cridge for help to mount a fundraising campaign. Their determination was the impetus behind the creation of a haven for destitute children in November 1872.

In a rented cottage, a Mrs. Todd was put in charge of the children. As their numbers grew, a larger building was rented at Blanshard and Rae, now Courtney. It officially became the B.C. Protestant Orphans' Home in 1873. Mary, Edward and Catherine devoted a great deal of effort to the cause for the rest of their lives: checking to see that the home was well run; that the children were happy, healthy and well clothed; and assisting often in raising the funds necessary to keep it in good order. Their enthusiasm and persistence led to a major breakthrough a number of years later.

In 1891, the retired policeman and former gold miner John George Taylor left all of his thirty-thousand dollar estate to the home. The bequest led to the purchase of a large piece of property on Hillside Avenue and construction of a new hundred-bed orphanage large enough to provide comfortable accommodation for all the homeless children. He made the donation because many of the children who found a home at the orphanage were the abandoned offspring of miners. The Cridges and Catherine Macdonald saw their prayers answered when the doors opened.

Decades later the orphanage was still operating. The Cridge Centre for the Family, on the same site, was named in honour of the two pioneers. At orphanage reunions many of those who lived there in years past still recall the loving care they received.[1] The building was converted in 1961 into a daycare centre and townhouses were built for families in crisis. The centre continues to offer family counselling and other care, playing a key role in Victoria's social welfare program. Its goal is to provide a range of community support for families and to give single parents a better chance in life. It is a lasting memorial to Edward and Mary Cridge, whose descendants continue to be involved with its operation.[2]

*   *   *

In the summer of 1868, Bishop Hills offered Dean Cridge the post of archdeacon, although it would not be in Victoria but on the mainland. Edward, who was strongly attached to the island city, discussed the matter with Mary, who expressed her preference for staying in Victoria. He also talked about the promotion with his old friend James Douglas and with other members of his congregation.

It is possible that Bishop Hills was trying to improve his stature in Victoria and felt this would be easier to accomplish with the much-loved Dean Cridge out of the way. The two men's differing views about the format for Christ Church services were becoming quite noticeable. The bishop favoured the elaborate High Church rites, while Dean Cridge, as he had always done, much preferred the simpler practices of the evangelical or Low Church. This was the same controversy he had faced back in England, but Cridge's beliefs were now more entrenched than ever. Despite his promotion to dean of Christ Church, he retained his lifelong dislike of religious ostentation, and he had often questioned the role of bishops and the expensive trappings of the ecclesiastical hierarchy.

Douglas recommended that Cridge remain in Victoria, advising him against going to the mainland. His congregation, many of them friends of long standing, also wanted him to stay. Edward did not want to leave the men and women who had become dear to him, the original settlers who had profoundly influenced the development and direction of Victoria in its early days. They still looked to Edward for guidance and advice and had not developed the same rapport with the bishop.

Edward's plans for a new home in James Bay, the one he had dreamed of for so long, were also now well advanced. It would never be the same for him on the mainland, and he knew it. Victoria was his home, much more so than any other place on earth. With the support of his congregation, Cridge turned down the bishop's offer to become an archdeacon. He could not have foreseen the major religious controversy that was soon to envelop him.

19

Troubles Brew in
the Cathedral

Disagreements between Dean Cridge and Bishop Hills increased as the two men continued to work in close proximity. Cridge was dean but as bishop, Hills often conducted services in Christ Church, and his own St. John's was nearby, his rectory around the corner. One of the issues that rankled Hills was the inclusion of Masonic rites at funerals, which the dean permitted. Cridge had always advocated freedom above most other things and wrote, "If I as a clergyman am allowed to read the church service uninterrupted, I have nothing to do with what follows."[1] The bishop, in contrast, was opposed to the addition of any extraneous material beyond the established funeral service and objected to the dean's position.

There had been an evangelical revival in the eighteenth century, followed by a High Church revival among Anglicans in the nineteenth century, which developed into Anglo-Catholicism. It became known as the Oxford movement because of its beginnings among those attending the famous university. Followers were also known as Tractarians because of the many tracts they wrote in support of their views. The division still exists, the elaborate ritual of the High Church resembling the Roman Catholic service, the Low Church service less formal and sometimes more evangelical.

Bishop Hills was attracted to ceremony and symbolism and some of the more elaborate acts of devotion typical of the Roman Catholic Church. The dean, for his part, disliked ritualism, from the genuflection whenever a minister passed the altar to directional posturing during a sermon. His resentment of these practices had built up over the years, but there is no evidence that he had previously objected publicly to it. He was by nature a quiet, non-confrontational man, although those who knew him well were aware of his convictions on this subject.

Early in December 1872, a special sermon sparked a religious crisis and a major social upheaval in Victoria. Three years had passed since Christ Church burned to the ground, and through the efforts of Dean Cridge and the congregation, as well as fundraising undertaken by the bishop, the church was now rebuilt. Bishop Hills declared the newly erected, more elaborate building his cathedral, the most important edifice in the diocese of Columbia. The bishop had until this time most frequently preached at St. John's, "the Iron Church."

On December 5, 1872, the new church was consecrated in a glittering celebration and ritual attended by church members and visitors from the mainland. Heads of other religions, municipal and government representatives, business and community leaders filled the pews of the new building. Bishop Hills, always a commanding figure, was in his element at the morning service, adorned in the magnificent robes used only for the most important religious celebrations. Mrs. Hills watched proudly as bells pealed, music from the large organ resounded to the vaulted ceiling, and the choir sang celebratory hymns. One of the highlights was the Twenty-third Psalm.

An eloquent speaker, the bishop looked confidently into the crowded pews and declared that the cathedral was now "a building set apart from profane and common uses and expropriated to the worship of the Most High."[2] Then he signed the official document making the church a cathedral. A special guest on this memorable occasion was Bishop Benjamin Morris of Oregon, who delivered the sermon.

The celebrations continued into the afternoon and evening, when Bishop Hills announced that he had asked Archdeacon William Reece from the mainland, the man appointed to the position Dean Cridge had refused, to take the pulpit in the evening. Christ Church Cathedral again was packed as the archdeacon paid tribute to all the special guests. With the formalities over, he began to preach, and gradually the congregation realized that he was developing a controversial theme. He advocated the adoption of ritualism in its most radical form, declaring that the Church of England had become cold and dead, and predicting its decay unless all the ritualism of the High Church was adopted in this new cathedral.

This was still Dean Cridge's church; most of the congregation were his parishioners, and were evangelical Christians. They listened politely but with a growing restlessness and concerned faces that betrayed their misgivings. The *Colonist* reported that it was a most extraordinary sermon for the occasion and shocked many of those in attendance. They listened with "ill-concealed impatience," said the paper.[3] When Dean Cridge strode forward to announce the next hymn, it was obvious from his stride and the expression on his usually passive face that he was furious. The dean could neither suppress his emotions nor hold back his words.

In a voice trembling with emotion, he cried, "I rise to protest against the views advocated by Archdeacon Reece. They are wrong and I would not again sit quietly and listen to their expression." For seventeen years he had presided over the Christ Church congregation, and this was the first time ritualism had been advocated. Immediately after his remarks, Christ Church was strangely silent. The many clergy in the cathedral were wide-eyed, aghast at this outburst in the midst of a service of consecration and celebration. Parishioners were initially as shocked as the members of the clergy, but as the dean's words sank in, they nodded in agreement. Then, slowly at first but with growing rancour, forgetting the sacred nature of the edifice and the celebration at hand, they gave vent to their own feelings by stamping and clapping.

The demonstration lasted for several minutes until Dean Cridge, having aired his anger, became calmer. Although he told the congregation that he hoped there would be no public demonstration over his protest, he must have realized that he had triggered a dispute with serious ramifications. In fact, his remarks ushered in a religious upheaval and a major crisis within the diocese and the community.

The archdeacon's sermon had been sanctioned by Bishop Hills, who knew full well that its sentiments were contrary to everything Dean Cridge believed. The bishop, however, must have expected the dean to accept the archdeacon's words without comment. He was using the occasion to reinforce his control as bishop of the diocese in his cathedral.

After the initial outburst, the bishop stood and faced the congregation, a stunned expression on his face. Behind him could be heard muttering among the white surplices in the chancellery. The public display of anger amounted to a revolt by one of his ministers on what was to have been his day of crowning glory. For the bishop what had just transpired was unbelievable and unbearable. He said nothing and then held a whispered conversation with his Oregon counterpart, the most influential figure in the Church on the Pacific coast and a startled witness to Bishop Hills' great embarrassment. The service was quickly brought to a close, and in the growing darkness of the chilly December evening the congregation gathered in groups outside the church to discuss the disturbing scene they had just witnessed.

Dean Cridge himself was by now well aware of what he had done. Some

Bishop Edward Cridge, c. 1875
(BC ARCHIVES, A-01196)

of his parishioners agreed with him, while others agreed in principle but argued that this had been the wrong time and place for him to have taken such a stand. The heated discussions ranged long on the church grounds as night descended. References to great religious dissenters in the times of Martin Luther and King Henry VIII could even be heard in the debates.

The Church of England was the largest denomination in the community but regarded as somewhat snooty and overbearing by those who practised other faiths. They found the discomfiture between Hills and Cridge amusing, viewing the crisis as a mere tempest in a teapot. It did, however, make for delightful gossip and speculation. The *Colonist* said the collection at the cathedral that night was a respectable amount, but in view of the clash over dogma, there was little consolation at Christ Church in the three hundred and seventeen dollars contributed from the morning and evening services. Meanwhile, the irony of what had happened was not lost on Bishop Demers. Hills, the man who had assailed the Catholic religion, its record on Vancouver Island and the motives of its bishop, had just been tripped up badly by some of the practices and rituals that were a regular part of Demers' services.

Archdeacon Reece hurriedly wrote a letter to the *Colonist*, printed on December 7. It said the object of the sermon had been to show "that adoration was the spontaneous act of the soul, quickened with spiritual life through communion with God." Reece insisted that ritualism continued to revive the Church, and in fact it was found to be a necessity in the Roman Catholic Church and the Jewish temple. He went into a long and involved religious argument that probably was well over the heads of most readers.

The *Colonist* pointed out that the rift was simply the long-lasting, divisive High Church–Low Church argument. One writer concluded that if people thought they were actually eating flesh and drinking blood that was up to them, and it was also up to an individual to grow nearer to God in his own way. The paper charged Reece, however, with being "indiscreet and in very bad taste."[4] Now a champion of Dean Cridge, the *Colonist* ran carefully selected letters favouring his position.

Although they could not avoid each other in person, there was soon little more than a published exchange of letters between Hills and Cridge. Meanwhile, the dean remained active in the community, presiding at the marriage of a prominent businessman, William Wilson, and Miss Emily Harris, the daughter of the mayor. Christmas was fast approaching, and there were the usual well-attended if somewhat tentative Christmas services. The dean also oversaw the holiday season at the hospital, the merriment of which was increased with the presentation of various gifts. Stafford and Hickens sent in a huge joint of roast beef, Hy Saunders a case of porter, Mr. Charles a fat goose and Gowen a keg of beer, according to the paper, which also noted that the Christmas display at the J. Moss candy and fruit store on Fort Street had the best holiday decorations, and the ten-foot decorated tree at the Toy Shop on Fort was right in season.[5]

The Hills-Cridge cold war smouldered for about a year. Many felt that with some give-and-take the row could have been settled, suggesting that the dean apologize for the timing of his charge and advising a careful resolution of differences, but neither party would initiate the reconciliation. The bishop had been greatly embarrassed by the affront, which had occurred at what should have been a highlight of his career. He considered Cridge's insubordination a personal insult, apart from the basic question of ritualism. The bishop had a point. Dean Cridge had known beforehand of Reece's High Church tendencies; he had heard his opinions previously during a service in Cowichan. Although Cridge perhaps did not expect them to be expressed during the consecration service, there could not have been a more dramatic time to vent his own feelings. To some, the dean's interjection seemed an intentional, well-thought-out move.

An exchange of letters between the two stubborn men failed to mend the breach, each refusing to change his position. Cridge made a half-hearted apology that he knew would not satisfy the bishop, who now wanted complete surrender to his authority. Cridge knew Hills would insist on nothing less if he were to retain his stature and authority as head of the Church in British Columbia.

Hills in turn told Cridge that he disagreed with Reece's sermon but felt Reece had said nothing that went beyond the limits of the liberty of opinion allowed and fostered in the Church of England. The public dissension had caused great pain to the visiting bishop of Oregon as well as to himself, said Hills, particularly the "stamping of feet, clapping of hands and other unseemly moves." He added that it was a "public scandal attacking him in the House of God." The bishop said that he could have taken much stricter action but had elected only to impose a severe censure on Cridge, because of his long service to the Church. The dean in response rejected the bishop's charges and censure, leaving Hills no room to manoeuvre.

They argued in great depth in a constant exchange of letters over the use of ritual in the order of service as practised by the tractarians and the much simpler evangelical services favoured by Cridge. Bishop Hills, through the Society for the Propagation of the Gospel, had encouraged an influx of High Church ministers and wanted to call a synod (a meeting of clergy) to discuss the issue of church ritual. Cridge feared Hills was attempting to impose ritualism on all the churches under his jurisdiction so he was opposed to the calling of a synod. He stated publicly that he respected the office of bishop as long as it did not trespass on the religious freedom of the clergy in the diocese. "Divine authority is the church itself, the actual congregation, and not in any man or order of men," he said. Hills disagreed and their differences were irreconcilable. Cridge viewed the argument as a duel between himself and the bishop and not a topic that should be taken to a synod, but Hills held the upper hand and called the first synod on December 23, 1873.

The crisis of authority broke into the open when Dean Cridge wrote to the *Colonist* on January 10, 1874, saying he had received too late a letter from Hills convening a diocesan synod to tackle the issue. He did not mince words, saying, "When one knows, not only by words but deeds, of the sword which, according to this view, is always hanging over a pastor's head, the very shadow of a bishop may well strike one with dread." He added, "A ministry carried on under, or by the side of such a power, becomes a ministry of horror and aversion rather than of love." The *Colonist* was happy to report fully on the now very public spat.

Cridge continued to challenge Hills' authority, maintaining that a diocese was a voluntary confederation of churches and that every congregation with an accepted parson was a complete church. In the Church of England this was heresy, and his words dashed any hope of reconciliation. He knew well that his contentions were anathema to the Church hierarchy and only his total and abject surrender to its power would be accepted. No matter how popular he was or how many good works he had done, the odds were against him in his dispute with the bishop. Within a month of his original outburst, Cridge faced eighteen separate charges in ecclesiastical court. He was accused of insubordination and contumacy (willful and/or obstinate resistance or disobedience to authority) and ordered to appear before the court at ten in the morning of September 10 in the Pandora Street church hall, the former Presbyterian church hall. The dean's popularity at Christ Church remained, however, and was more than evident when the Cridge faction swept all the posts in parish secular elections in April.

Edward and Mary, despite what they knew was coming, enjoyed the pleasant summer in Victoria, but the difficult days of September arrived all too soon. As the ecclesiastical court convened, Bishop Hills sat on the panel along with the assessors: Archdeacon Woods, the Reverend Mason, and the county court judges O'Reilly and Bushby.

The *Colonist* charged that the panel was Hills' hand-picked kangaroo court and that its makeup might be in accordance with Church law but clashed with the public's idea of justice and presented a "repulsive picture." At its indignant best, the paper claimed that if anything like this were tried in connection with a common or civil law case, "the whole community would rise up against it as monstrous, as wicked, as destructive of its dearest liberties." The paper further stated that the sympathy and support already shown to the well-loved pastor was proof that Dean Cridge would not be deserted in "this hour of his extremity and trouble."[6]

A large crowd, mostly women, waited to enter when the proceedings opened. For the religious and the non-religious alike, this was a diversion from their everyday activities. The *Colonist* reported the event in great detail, explaining that there was a uniformed policeman at the door equipped with handcuffs and wearing a revolver. The editor said that feelings ran so high on the issue that a heated argument had prompted one person to commit arson. This had happened a few hours earlier when "some evil disposed person" torched the hay sheds behind Bishop Hills' residence.

The crowd listened attentively as the eighteen charges against Dean Cridge were read. He was accused of refusing to acknowledge the bishop's authority, obstructing the bishop's functions and treating Hills' censure with contempt, and although only words had been used in the altercation in Christ Church, he also faced a count of brawling in the church. The other charges included some instances of obstruction when he refused to turn over certain documents. Dean Cridge challenged the proceedings as illegal and irregular, and the crowd applauded loudly as he admitted to having made mistakes but argued that he had committed no crime. He played to their sympathy as he asked those present to pray for him.

The lawyers dug into old books, cited ancient laws and arguments, the details of Letters Patent and questions of theology. The crowd gathered that the lawyers' convoluted references to Church disturbances in far-off Natal in Africa and Tasmania in the South Pacific had some bearing on the situation, but they were far from sure exactly what. The examination was sufficiently dull that the second day opened to a much smaller house, although the *Colonist*, revelling in the embarrassment of the bishop and his Church, gave columns of coverage to the hearing. The third day was much the same, with the dean still challenging the hearing's legality.

The fourth day of the trial was livelier, and the crowd once again cheered and stamped their feet when Cridge alleged that Hills had seceded from the Church of England by usurping the powers of Queen Victoria. Stating that there was no sense in continuing the trial under these conditions, Cridge announced abruptly that he was withdrawing from the hearing. The sudden move stunned the judges and had the watchers gasping. Cridge stood and strode dramatically from the hall, accompanied by his supporters. The surprised court held a hurried and whispered discussion but soon realized there was nothing they could do about the situation and adjourned. Cridge's departure signalled a new direction in his argument with the bishop, and his intentions soon became evident.

20

The Reformed
Episcopal Church

The *Colonist*, more anxious than ever to support Dean Cridge, learned
he had talked with those close to him in the congregation about a
new church affiliation. The paper subsequently ran several stories drawing attention to the recent growth in Canada of the Reformed Episcopal
Church, which had been introduced in Toronto two years previously. This
had followed a split there at Toronto's Holy Trinity Church over the same
issue. The *Colonist* stated, "It is the tyrannical spirit and Ritualistic tendencies of the Bishops that are doing the mischief there — much the same as
here, in fact."[1] Although he stated nothing publicly, Cridge had indicated
to his congregation that he might ally himself with another church if he
were forced to leave the Church of England. In Canada at this time there
were already three or four Reformed Episcopal parishes.

Advance notice of a September 18 decision in Cridge's trial guaranteed a crowd that overflowed from the hall onto Pandora Street. Bishop Hills, eager to end the session, quickly announced that the dean had been found guilty of sixteen of the eighteen charges, including all the major ones. The bishop was interrupted by yelling and hissing. The uproar grew when the bishop declared it his "painful office" to suspend Cridge as dean of Christ Church. The bishop said he had no intention of removing Cridge permanently, even though the decision was his to make. Hills stated that while he waited for Cridge's decision, a portion of Christ Church's income would go to support the Cridge family.[2]

As they hurried out of the hall, some of the dean's supporters, angry at the outcome of the trial, tolled the bell that still hung in the old Presbyterian church hall. A crowd gathered and milled around outside, giving three cheers for their vicar followed by shouts of "God bless him." The *Colonist* stated that the audience would never forget the spontaneous support Cridge received during and after the trial and immediately launched a spectacular campaign on his behalf. No condemnation of Hills was too great. The paper said the synod's "act of tyranny is universally condemned," although few people beyond Vancouver Island and British Columbia ever heard of it. "No one but a lunatic or a man drunk with power would have acted as the Bishop has done,"[3] it declared, claiming that Dean Cridge's suspension was "a wicked, flagrant, un-Christian outrage on a man as guileless as a little child and purer than gold double-refined."[4] Only days later, on September 21, Cridge's right to preach as a Church of England minister was revoked. He was stoic, but this schism in the Church to which he had devoted much of his life was a major heartbreak. Mary was steadfast by his side throughout the ordeal.

The congregation wondered and worried about what might happen with the pulpit empty the following Sunday. In the interim, the *Colonist*, flirting with inciting conflict, claimed that any attempt to occupy Cridge's place would be resisted. While some wept about what was happening to their church, others found the conflict between the dean and the bishop a rather interesting event in their usually quiet lives. After all, there had not been this much excitement in Victoria since the invasion of the gold miners fourteen years earlier.

Tension hung in the air as a crowd gathered in front of Christ Church on Sunday morning. At quarter to eleven, the Sunday school children and their teachers marched from the Pandora Street hall to the church, as was their custom. Then, as a hushed silence fell over the congregation, Cridge walked quietly through the throng. He went into the vestry, donned his robes of office and, as the choir sang the processional, took his normal place in the apse of the church. The *Colonist* described the scene outside: "The number of young, athletic looking men present was very large, and here and there on Church Hill were groups of Muscular Christians, quietly awaiting the course of events."[5] Tension mounted when there was a shout that the bishop's carriage had left the rectory, with Mrs. Hills sitting primly beside the primate, appearing unconcerned although she must have been tightly wound. Instead of making for the cathedral, however, the horse and carriage turned towards Esquimalt, and word quickly spread that His Lordship was going to officiate at St. Paul's Church at the naval base. Everyone breathed a sigh of relief, for no one wanted the scene that would have occurred had the bishop carried out his intention of conducting all morning and evening services at Christ Church.

Inside, Cridge began the service at precisely eleven o'clock with wife Mary closely watching, her face showing pride and affection. He made no mention of the bishop's edict as he delivered a sermon based on the 122nd Psalm. It was an impressive performance, as he did not betray his feelings except for his choice of the closing hymn. Its last line was "Defiance to the Gates of Hell." The congregation sang with gusto and the walls rang with the sound of their voices. Christ Church was full for the evening service, again conducted by Dean Cridge.

The bishop, however, immediately applied for an injunction to remove the dissident from the cathedral. It was heard September 22, 1874, before Supreme Court Chief Judge Matthew Begbie, who was about to depart for

England. While tough in sentencing, Begbie administered justice in a fair fashion in the rough early days of the colony. He did not deserve the nickname later given to him, the "Hanging Judge." Begbie personally preferred Cridge to Hills. He listened to a summation of all the evidence, mercifully spared the problems of Natal and Tasmania, before he adjourned to consider his verdict, feeling there had been misunderstanding on both sides. He called on both men to try to find a resolution. The lawyers met but there was no reconciliation. On September 24, Begbie found for Hills, and by law Dean Cridge was now forbidden to enter the cathedral, the church he had twice seen built from the ground up.

Senator Macdonald called on Judge Begbie a couple of days after the verdict was delivered, berating him for the decision. The judge, who was a friend of the minister, sent Dean Cridge a cheque for twelve hundred dollars to cover the expenses of the trial, but it was never cashed. A public subscription had collected fifteen hundred, more than sufficient to cover all his costs.

On Sunday morning, Judge Augustus F. Pemberton, one of the Christ Church wardens, walked up Church Hill and turned over the keys of the church to the Reverend F. B. Gribbell, the very nervous new rector. There was not the same large crowd as there had been previously, but Gribbell expected some kind of protest and wondered exactly what the group of about sixty men and boys standing close to the doors might do. As soon as he opened them he knew. The men dashed in and began snatching Bibles, hymn books, stools, cushions and other items from the pews. They were removing possessions from their regular pews or on behalf of other members of the congregation who had decided to leave the church with the Reverend Cridge.

When the main rush abated, the Reverend Gribbell looked over an almost empty church. The *Colonist* counted a lonely handful of twelve regular members and thirteen strangers. The pastor gamely began a service but there was no sexton, no organist and only two men in the choir stalls. He delivered a distracted short sermon before bringing the service to an end while a continuous stream of people arrived to remove their belongings. The Reverend Gribbell made another brave attempt to hold a service at the cathedral that evening. An organist had been found, and the music sounded out over the heads of a huddled group of twenty-two people. They tried a hymn, faltered, and the service was over, but not until a few more stragglers arrived to take more of their possessions from the almost bare pews. Meanwhile, the Reverend Cridge, his family and many of his parishioners were worshipping together with the Reverend Jenns at nearby St. John's, formerly the bishop's home parish.

For days, members of Cridge's congregation continued to enter Christ Church carrying portmanteaus, valises and baskets to cart off what remained of the church furnishings. A carriage arrived and departed with a strip of red carpet. Members of the congregation felt it was unjust that Cridge had been forced to surrender the church to which he had been devoted for so long. These were people who had put up the bulk of the money to build Christ Church, and they believed it was theirs. They were particularly annoyed that they must leave behind the organ, which had been purchased through the sustained fundraising efforts of the women of the parish.

Technically, Bishop Hills had won, but his authority and prestige had suffered another very public and damaging setback from which he never fully recovered. The good he did in his years in Victoria and the province were lost to some extent, undermined by the Cridge affair as well as the printing of his early report with its caustic, ill-considered comments about the colony and Bishop Demers.

The *Colonist* remained in the midst of the fray. There were demands that Bishop Hills be removed. Letters to the editor claimed that Cridge was the victim of tyrannical hirelings and Hills' ritualistic tendencies and persecution, which seemed "determined to push the matter to extremities and involve himself and the Church in one common ruin."[6] No exaggeration, it seemed, was too great.

21

A New Church Is Born

The Reverend Cridge, no longer a dean, broke the stand-off with the announcement of an important meeting to be held on October 29 in the Pandora Street hall. At least three-quarters of the Christ Church congregation filled the seats. A feeling of great expectation was in the air as their friend and pastor explained that for him there was no turning back. He said that he had no option but to submit to the Supreme Court ruling. With difficulty, carefully holding his emotions in check, he said he knew his only option was to sever his long relationship with the Church of England. The crowd, some of them also near tears, applauded his sentiment.

Some close friends had guessed what was coming as he explained he must seek another church affiliation that would more closely reflect his views and his hopes for the future. He admitted to his congregation that as yet he knew little about the Reformed Episcopal Church, but he had been in touch with them, and it seemed that this relatively new organization was in tune with his beliefs. Its ministers used an evangelical and not a ritualistic approach to worship services. The Reformed Episcopal Church had originated with the assistant bishop of Kentucky, George David Cummins, who left his church in November 1873, because of ritualism that had crept into the Protestant Episcopal Church in the United States. After a meeting in New York of like-minded people, the new church was created on October 27, 1874. Cummins maintained the new church members were not revolutionaries but reformers, or restorers, "removing the corruption of the present."[1] This was the philosophy for which the Reverend Cridge was looking. He told the congregation there were as yet only five of these churches in Canada, three in New Brunswick and two in Toronto.

Cridge's sincerity and belief were contagious, and the former Christ Church faithful followed him in a body. They prayed with him, asking God to bless their endeavours. These were residents of a new country, and many had already broken away from their countries of origin when they left Europe to find a place in a new world. They were now breaking with the past again — a past some of their families had been a part of for many generations. In this new country they decided to start a new church with a creed they endorsed, friends they respected and a pastor they loved and admired.

The new congregation was made up of the elite of Victoria, people who had been the backbone of Christ Church. They were the pioneers and founders of the colony. Amongst the two hundred and fifty names listed as members of the new congregation were the former governor James Douglas, surveyor J. D. Pemberton, Senator William Macdonald, Dr. John Helmcken, Mayor Thomas Harris, and the U.S. consul Allen Francis. Many of these names are well remembered as districts or streets, in or near Victoria. Another member was Richard Carr, whose daughter Emily Carr was to become one of British Columbia's best known artists and writers.

Enthusiasm ran high as four hundred people packed the Pandora Street hall for the first Sunday morning service early in November. The evening service drew almost as many. Because of a seating shortage, the congregation decided immediately to spend three hundred dollars to build a temporary gallery to hold another seventy people until a new church could be built.

Although the congregation included no one with the millions of Miss Burdett-Coutts, who had financed the first Church of England diocese in the province, James Douglas stepped in with a donation of land. He offered two lots on Humboldt Street for the new church as well as one-tenth of the cost of construction, to a maximum of ten thousand dollars. Senator Macdonald offered a choice of one of three city lots and a donation of five thousand. After careful consideration, a church committee chose the Humboldt location. It was close to the harbour and the mudflats that were later to become the site of the palatial Empress Hotel.

Construction began quickly on the church, designed by the engineer and architect John Teague. Like many other Victorians, Teague was English-born and had come to the colony from California with the miners in 1858. The building's simplicity was in keeping with the Reverend Cridge's wishes. The exterior was built with native Douglas fir, in the Gothic style, decorative but not overdone. Much of the interior was finished in California redwood, and the roof beams, flooring and pews were made with the wooden pegs typical of pioneer carpentry. The church interior glowed with the warmth of polished natural wood. Stained glass windows honouring Douglas and other famous local men were installed later. The price for the new church was $9,700 and, with furnishings, the cost for the whole project was $12,000.

In addition to the land and cash, Douglas also provided a new church organ. It arrived in Victoria in 1875. Built in 1827 in Boston by Thomas A. Appleton, it had an interesting history before its arrival in Victoria, having been brought around Cape Horn to San Francisco, possibly the first church organ in that city. After some years in the California city, it was sold and shipped to Victoria. Over the years it has been repaired and refinished several times, and it remains today the centrepiece of the Church of Our Lord.

The highly enthusiastic *Colonist* gave the new church its whole-hearted support and provided its readers with a blow-by-blow account of construction progress. The coverage was driven more by the paper's dislike of Bishop Hills and his treatment of the Reverend Cridge than by any great religious devotion. Yet many non-churchgoers were among the residents who gave a cheer for the breakaway, stand-up-for-what-you-believe spirit and convictions of the dissenters. *Colonist* readers learned that those who had volunteered to build the gallery at Pandora Street had also done much of the work at the new church. A communion cloth and silver service were donated along with other gifts and, most importantly, cash. The *Colonist* suggested that Christ Church was doing its best just to hold on to its Sunday school pupils. It then devoted space to reprint an entire Cridge sermon, offering reprints free of charge to its readers. Meanwhile a cathedral spokesman maintained a stiff upper lip, contending that the weekly offerings showed little decline following the Cridge affair.

When the new church was ready for occupancy, legend would have it that the Reverend Cridge led his congregation, marching shoulder to shoulder with children perched on some of them, proudly and defiantly down Church Hill, their voices raised in rousing hymns — a scene one might expect to find in a Hollywood biblical epic. No doubt they celebrated spiritually but not physically, although the vision of a march presents a dramatic, symbolic myth. Cynics jibed that the new Church of Our Lord, the name chosen by Cridge for his church, had been kicked down to the bottom of Church Hill by the cathedral. Writing some years later, Emily Carr suggested that "Victorians chose High or Low, whichever comforted them most."[2]

Throughout his trials and tribulations, Cridge kept up with his regular duties, no matter where they took him. He had been a frequent visitor to Woodside in Sooke and continued to visit the Muir family there. They had become friends, and his closeness to them included officiating at the death of a daughter-in-law and then the marriage in 1874 of their oldest son, John Muir Jr. Their long friendship ended when the vicar conducted the funeral of the eighty-three-year-old pioneer, who died in 1883. Muir had been one of the prominent early settlers; his achievements included serving in the first Victoria legislative assembly, serving as a magistrate and developing a thriving lumber export business, which expanded to become a shipping company using locally built vessels.

On February 12, 1875, the Reverend Cridge received a letter from the Hudson's Bay Company, which apparently still owned the parsonage building. It stated he was to terminate all connections with the parsonage and the land around it. The family had already returned to Sellindge Cottage.

* * *

January 16, 1876, was a proud day for the many friends and Victoria pioneers who formed the founding congregation of the Church of Our Lord. A crowd gathered early, standing to admire the attractive wooden building. Some had helped build it with their own hands, others had raised funds, and still others had provided decorations and furnishings. For long hours during 1875, to make the Church of Our Lord their own, the congregation had devoted their efforts and all their spare time to building their church. Now it was a reality. Their dearest wish was to see the doors swing open for the first time, and on this cold January day they watched, delighted with their achievement. Quietly, quickly and with some awe they filled the pews. There was standing room only inside and worshippers spilled out onto the street. The Reverend Cridge blessed the church and the congregation and read the opening prayers. The Reverend Mr. McGregor preached an eloquent sermon. Then the organ rang out, voices were raised lustily and triumphantly, and tears, this time of joy, streamed down the faces of many.

The Reverend Cridge found great satisfaction in the fact that the Church of Our Lord's first organist was Fanny Macdonald Leech, who had arrived on the "bride ship" *Tynemouth* in 1862. This inaugural service was a great celebration, one completely free of the trappings of ritualism, just as the

Reverend Cridge had always wanted. The *Colonist* reported that the six hundred people who packed the church comprised the largest congregation ever assembled in Victoria.[3] The names, position or occupation, and the number in each family are still listed at the church. These are some of the people who went down the hill from the High Church to the Low Church to become founding members of the Church of Our Lord.

First Congregation at the Church of Our Lord, 1876

NAME	POSITION/ OCCUPATION	NUMBER IN FAMILY
Thos. T. C. Allat	Contractor	6
Mr. & Mrs. Andaun & family		2
Mrs. Blinkhorn		1
Mrs. Carter Booth		2
J. H. Carmichael		5
Richard Carr	Merchant	7
Coote Chambers		3
Mrs. Couves		2
John Crowther		3
Capt. Devareux	Dry Dock	4
E. Dickinson		4
Sir James Douglas	Former governor	5
Jno. Dutnall		1
Capt. Ella		5
Judge Elliott		3
I. Englehardt	Agent	5
Mrs. Fanny		1
Mr. & Mrs. E. Fawcett		2
Mr. & Mrs. R. W. Fawcett		2
Thomas L. Fawcett		1
John Flewin		3
Thos. Flewin	Govt. Official	3
Hon. Allen Francis	U.S. Consul	3
Geo. Frye	Customs	4
Alex. A. Green	Banker	4
Mayor Harris		4
Dennis Harris	Civil Engineer	3
Mdm. & Mdlles. Hartnagle	Hotelkeeper	3

NAME	POSITION/ OCCUPATION	NUMBER IN FAMILY
Chas. Haywood	Contractor	3
Wm. Heathorn	Merchant	5
Dr. J. S. Helmcken		5
T. N. Hibben	Bookseller	6
D. W. Higgins	Editor	4
Robt. Jenkinson	Contractor	5
Stephen Jones	Hotelkeeper	3
J. L. Kennedy		1
Alfred J. Langley	Druggist	6
Wm. Leigh	Town Clerk	4
Peter Lester & Booths		4
Capt. & Mrs. Lewis	Hudson's Bay Co.	2
Richard Lewis	Mayor	3
W. J. Macdonald	Senator	6
Mr. Mahood	Surveyor	3
R. Maynard	Photographer	2
Mrs. McTavish & Family		3
Capt. William Mitchell	Hudson's Bay Co.	1
Capt. & Mrs. Moffatt		2
Capt. H. Moffat	Hudson's Bay Co.	4
Gac. Morrison	Druggist	5
Capt. Mouat	[Hudson's Bay Co.]	5
Mrs. Nesbitt		4
Samuel Nesbitt		4
Wm. Newbury		7
Mrs. Dr. Nicholles		2
T. Nicholson		3
R. Offerhaus		2
Digby Palmer	Prof. Music	5
B. W. Pearse	Provincial Government	3
Judge Pemberton		4
Joseph D. Pemberton	Surveyor General	6
Madame Pettibeau		1
Wm. P. Sayward	Lumber Merchant	3
Capt. Swanson	Hudson's Bay Co.	2
Mr. & Mrs. Henry Thain		2
Cornelius Thorn		2
Col. Rich. Wolfenden	Queen's Printer	4
J. J. Young	Govt. Official	2

The long confrontation with Bishop Hills was over. In the years to come, the bishop conducted his services filled with the ritualism he loved in Christ Church at the top of the hill. In the Church of Our Lord, now affiliated with the Reformed Episcopal Church, the Reverend Edward Cridge provided the simple services he loved, and delivered the basic Christian messages his congregation had come to expect.

The man who had fought Bishop Hills was elected missionary bishop of the Reformed Episcopal Church at the General Council in Chicago in 1875. He was consecrated bishop on July 16, 1876 in Emmanuel Church in Ottawa. While there attending a meeting of Reformed Episcopal Church ministers he was elected as a delegate to represent the church at the convocation in the Free Church of England to be held in England on August 20. The Free Church of England was formed in 1863 and was affiliated with the Reformed Episcopal Church in the U.S., which was formed in 1873.[4] In all Cridge was away from Victoria for three months, returning on October 4, 1876.

It was to be his only visit to England, the land he and Mary had left twenty-two years earlier. He enjoyed his stay, visiting almost forgotten friends and college mates from his early years. However, England was no longer home for him, and he returned to Victoria with the certainty in his heart that this was his place in the world.

22

Marifield and Emily Carr

J ust before Cridge's appointment as bishop, he and Mary, knowing
their church was now on a firm footing, looked once again at building
a home of their own that would comfortably accommodate their family. It
would also complement his stature as the leader of a new church. His
dream of a home became a reality midway through 1875, when Marifield
was completed for $2,337. As time went by, Marifield became the home
that Edward and Mary had always wanted, furnished to their own tastes
and accommodating the new traditions that had become a part of their life
in Victoria.

Edward now devoted more time to his family. He was responsible for
only one church with a well-organized congregation. He visited other
churches under his jurisdiction on a regular basis, but he was no longer
heavily involved with the social responsibilities that had filled his younger

Marifield, home of Edward and Mary Cridge, c. 1900
(CITY OF VICTORIA ARCHIVES, PR76-1269)

years. Instead, he had time to enjoy the exploits of his four daughters: Mary, now fifteen years of age; Rhoda, aged ten; Ellen, eight; and Maude, seven. He went skating with them, took pleasure in gardening and helped with the haying. He comments in his diary that he fell off a horse but was not hurt. He says he went "shopping with wife" and makes several references such as "assisted at machine with wife" and "helping wife with machine." The family had household help, and it is unlikely they worked at an early washing machine or operated the butter churn. What the machine was remains a mystery that historians cannot answer.

As well as the four girls, the Cridges' home continued to accommodate Elizabeth Cridge and the house staff along with frequent visitors. The house was well situated near the shore of the Strait of Juan de Fuca, with the peaks of Washington's Olympic Mountains in the distance. Marifield was at the end of a driveway lined with laurels, and the two-storey home was fronted with roses. It featured two tall chimneys and a front veranda. Over the years Cridge planted an orchard, a vegetable plot, and flowers that he had known in the gardens of England. Also on the property were a barn and two fields, in which their cow Colie and the horse Charlie grazed. As the children grew older, a tennis court was added, the first in the city of Victoria.

Many happy celebrations took place at Marifield. One retired English naval officer, Captain W. H. Heeley, recalled years later that although he was far from home he had spent a very merry Christmas with the Cridges in 1882. The tennis court set up on the front lawn became very popular. It attracted Robert Service, the bard of the Yukon, when he was working briefly in a Victoria bank, and often heard on the court at the time was the quip, "It's your service, Service."[1]

The Cridges' neighbours across the street were Richard Carr and his large family. The Carrs and the Cridges were close friends and shared similar lifestyles. Carr was an English-born businessman, a prominent city merchant and an early arrival in Victoria. He imported provisions, wines and cigars for his store in the growing commercial district on Wharf Street. His daughter Emily Carr, who later became a world-renowned artist, played in the fields with her sisters and the Cridge girls, Mary and Ellen. The children remembered running to open the gate for Mrs. Cridge so that she could drive off in the wide family carriage. Mary usually did the driving, with Bishop Cridge as the passenger, when they went to town to work on one of their many projects.

The Cridge home was a religious one but nonetheless a lively one. As was common in the nineteenth century, the family received visitors at home every Thursday evening. Bishop Cridge often entertained by playing his cello, accompanied by daughter Ellen, affectionately known as "Nell," on the piano. Today's Marifield Avenue once was the driveway into the Cridge home, at first called Cridge Avenue.

*　*　*

Bishop Edward Cridge, playing the cello, c. 1900
(BC ARCHIVES, A-01201 / PHOTO: SKENE LOWE)

Emily Carr had fond memories of Bishop Cridge, Marifield, the Church of Our Lord and the quiet Sundays of her childhood. Born in Victoria in 1870, Emily was the second youngest in a family of nine. She was five when the Reverend Cridge built Marifield and the Cridge family moved in across the street. She lovingly recalls the days of her childhood in her memoir, *The Book of Small*, in which she describes the people, customs, lifestyle, disputes and sorrows that made up life in a city that, slightly more than thirty years earlier, had been but a fort with sentries confronting a wilderness of trees.[2]

The Carrs were among the first to acquire extensive property in the area just west of Beacon Hill Park. Their fields abutted the Cridge acreage, and initially there was common use of Carr Road. Both families had shared the same sorrow, with the deaths of young children claimed by epidemics. The Cridges had lost four children, three sons and a daughter, while the Carrs had watched three sons die. Despite the grief suffered in these tragic times both families remained firm in their faith, and like all the devout citizens of early Victoria, they practised their religion every day of the week. Each morning at quarter to nine, the patriarch sat in the parlour in a wicker seat known as the "Praying Chair" to conduct prayers for the family and servants before he left for business and the children headed off for school. On Sunday, almost the entire day was given up to worship. Emily recounts in detail the typical Sundays of this era, and we can surmise that her family's activities were similar to those of the family next door at Marifield.

The routine actually began on Saturday night when Bong, the Chinese servant, began the preparation of meals to be consumed on Sunday. The weekly roast was cooked in a tin oven and served cold the following day. With a large family it was a large roast. Emily's father maintained that a roast under twenty pounds was just not worth cooking, as all the juice would run out. Saturday was also bath night. A large wooden tub was brought in and placed in the middle of the kitchen floor. All the large pots were filled with water and sat heating on a stove until emptied into the tub as the children, one after the other, were soaked, soaped and scrubbed. They were then rinsed and wrapped in soft, warm towels. All the children's toys and books were then put away before bedtime. The family arose at seven o'clock on Sunday.

The long round of sober Sabbath observances began with family prayers, which were a little longer than on weekdays. The Carrs were not wed to any particular church in the early days, Richard preferring the Presbyterian service in the morning — partly because he was slightly deaf and knew he could get a seat near the front — while his wife went to the evening service at the Church of Our Lord. The children all participated in the two-mile morning walk to church and attended both the Church of

Our Lord and the Presbyterian Church. Emily recalled walking through heat, rain, sleet or snow depending on the season, and listening to all the bells calling parishioners to worship. She remarked particularly on the chimes from the cathedral atop Church Hill. There was little other sound on those silent Sundays except for the clip-clop of horses' hooves.

The Church of Our Lord had neither bells nor chimes, but Emily enjoyed it, finding it mellow and beautiful. She explained that there were four splendid chandeliers with round, wide tin reflectors that shone light from the gas jets up to the raftered roof. She was intrigued by a lady in a red velvet bonnet who played hymns on the organ. Perhaps she was the same one from the bride ship that Bishop Cridge had been so pleased to have join the church. The lady accompanied a mixed choir dressed in various styles of Sunday best, not gowned in snow-white surplices like the cathedral singers. Emily always sang along with them. She thought it appropriate that the mellow little church had a gentle, mild leader like Bishop Cridge.

She wrote: "He wore a long black gown with a long white surplice over it. His immense puff sleeves were caught in at the wrists by black bands and fluted out again in little white frills around his wrists. There was a dimple on each knuckle of his hands. He was a wide man and looked wider in his surplice, especially from our pew, which was close up under the pulpit. He looked very high above us and every time he caught his breath his beard hoisted and waved out."[3] She found him soft-spoken, especially when he gave the blessing, which she felt was the most important part of the service. Emily recalled how Bishop Cridge always carefully scanned the sheets on which his sermon was written to make sure he had not missed anything before he said a gentle "Amen." Emily thought that he gave the blessing, "just as if he was taking it straight from God and giving it to us." The Bishop, she said, "was very holy," and "his eyes were blue, as if by his perpetual contemplation of Heaven they had taken its colour. His gentle voice, vague and distant, came from up there too. His plump hands were transparent against the clerically black vest."[4]

Despite Emily's obvious pleasure in the Reverend Cridge's preaching voice, his soft, sonorous tones could cause problems for those who allowed their thoughts to drift during his sermons. Its effects had proved mortifying a few years earlier for two very devout spinster sisters, Catherine and Anna Penrice, who had come from England to work at the Anglican girls' school. One admitted shame-faced that she had nodded off during the service. They had a stool of penitence at their home and she spent a half-hour on it in atonement.

For the Carrs there was always the walk back home for noontime Sunday dinner. The menu never varied. It was always cold roast beef served with potato salad and pickled cabbage, followed by apple pie with lots of thick Devonshire cream. After the meal, Richard Carr asked his children who remembered best what had been said and what was the message in the sermon they had heard that morning. Sister Dede usually gave a scattered summation. Alice remembered the text, but Lizzie could be depended on to go through all of it. Emily recalled that she usually had nothing left to say and got away with noting that everything had already been covered by her sisters.

While her father lay down for his afternoon nap and her mother read from the Good Book, Dede, Emily's older sister, took her siblings to the nearby Cridge home, where she taught a Sunday school class. While waiting for her sister to finish the class, Emily sat in the large living room where she could not take her eyes off the old woman who always sat there. "The Bishop's invalid sister sat in the room all the time. Her cheeks were hollow, she had sharp eyes with red rims, sat by the fire, wore a cap and coughed, not because she had to, but just to remind us that she was watching and listening," she wrote.[5] The bishop's sister, Elizabeth, who had worked tirelessly to aid Edward and Mary with the school and the hospital and in counselling parishioners, suffered from severe arthritis in her later years and was confined to a chair much of the time. She was very fond of young children and still enjoyed their company, especially the Carr girls. She lived at Marifield until her death in 1890 at the age of seventy.

After Sunday school there was a traditional family walk around the property. Emily's father had originally bought ten acres, and he led his brood through the family fields, which were dotted with flowers for much of the spring and summer months. The Cridges and the Carrs planted many of the same flowers, and they were rewarded by a profusion of blooms: stocks, phlox, lilies, violets, Canterbury bells, foxgloves, delphiniums, poppies, flags, sweet william, heliotrope, snapdragons, pinks, daisies and roses. Mrs. Carr always held the hand of little Dick tightly during the walk. He was her only surviving son. Emily wrote that she and her sisters found the stroll boring and tiring, and they would sooner have played with the Cridge girls, but this of course was not permissible on Sunday.

Bong came to the Carr home twice on Sunday to milk the family cow, usually singing to it in a high-pitched voice, almost the only sign of anything resembling work that was done during the day. The Carrs, like most of their neighbours, did not finish their Sabbath observances until well into the evening, when there was again a lengthy reading from the big family bible. The children's eyes drooped as the bible study went on and on. Fortunately at nine o'clock there was salvation. With a roar that could be heard all over the town, the gun at the naval base at Esquimalt boomed out the nightly signal, the pages of the Bible were carefully closed, and the long Sunday ritual that had begun at seven in the morning was over.

23

The Passing of
Three Pioneers

Noone outside of his immediate family felt greater sorrow when Sir James Douglas died on August 2, 1877, than Mary and Edward. He was the man who had met them at water's edge when they arrived at the small, desolate fort twenty-two years earlier. Over the years they had developed much affection for the former fur trader, who became a knighted statesman in the land he had led for so long. In the building of British Columbia, he was the cornerstone.

Douglas had never tired of looking at the beauty of Victoria, and he died shortly after being taken for a carriage ride around the waterfront. His son-in-law, Dr. Helmcken, was called to care for him, but when he arrived Douglas had slumped forward in his favourite chair and was gone. He lived a very full seventy-four years, leaving his wife, a son, and

Funeral of Sir James Douglas at the Church of Our Lord, Victoria. The parsonage is the large building to the right; Christ Church with its tower is in the background

(BC ARCHIVES, A-01266 / PHOTO: FREDERICK DALLY)

four daughters, one of them living in England and one in the United States. Cecilia, the daughter who married Dr. Helmcken, died years earlier, in 1865. The Douglases had suffered the deaths at a young age of seven of their thirteen children. Despite this sorrow, Douglas had always carried on doing his best for Victoria and its people. Bishop Cridge recalled talking to Douglas the Sunday before he died. The old ex-governor told Cridge his "heart rose in gratitude to God for his love and the goodness displayed in his works."[1]

While Douglas lay in state at home, a cross on his chest, Bishop Cridge worked on the memorial arrangements and dealt with the many organizations and individuals who wanted to take part in the funeral procession. Visitors came from the mainland, and others travelled long distances by buggy on the Island to be in Victoria on August 7. Many wore black armbands. Four black-draped horses pulled the hearse from Douglas's home to the Church of Our Lord, which was full to overflowing.

Bishop Cridge preached a relatively brief sermon.[2] The casket was borne from the church, and a procession, led by a naval band and accompanied by more than one hundred sailors and marines, wound through crowd-lined streets to Ross Bay Cemetery. As church bells tolled throughout Victoria, the hearse made its slow journey, followed by sixty carriages and hundreds of marchers whose numbers filled the road for nearly a mile. The service for the dead was read at the graveside, and a military contingent fired a salute while the boom of naval guns could be heard in the distance. Bishop Cridge's personal farewell, which followed the sermon in the order of service, was a fitting one for his admired and respected patron.

At Christ Church Cathedral, special tribute was also paid to Douglas. Archdeacon Henry P. Wright said he was the dominant man in early B.C. history and would be remembered for his great contribution, as a "gallant, honest, upright, far-seeing ruler." The archdeacon also mentioned that "Douglas' affection for Cridge was his main reason for leaving Christ Church, but he had remained a financial contributor to the Church of England and had always treasured his prayer book." Accolades poured in from across the country and around the world, and even the *Colonist* had glowing praise and fine words for the man it had targeted so often. It reported that the entire province was in tears, as flags flew at half-mast and many buildings were hung with black drapery. One of Douglas's final acts had been to give Bishop Cridge five hundred dollars to pay a debt at the Church of Our Lord.

✻ ✻ ✻

Life went on and the bishop's eldest daughter, Mary, became friends with a prominent local banker, James Cran, whom she married in 1880 at the Church of Our Lord. Bishop Cridge performed the ceremony, and many from the congregation joined in the celebrations. The newlyweds lived in Victoria for only a short time before James Cran was transferred to San Francisco. Later they moved to Ashcroft and eventually retired to Quamichan Lake, near Duncan. One of their two sons, Duncan, became a well-known pioneer in the community of Fort St. John, in northern British Columbia.

Another young man who visited the Cridge home during the ensuing years was Thomas Herbert Laundy, who came to play tennis at Marifield. Thomas, born in London and educated at King's College in Kent, had gone to San Francisco to work in a bank and while there married a woman named Bertha. He transferred to Victoria in 1889, where he worked at the Bank of British Columbia, the forerunner of the Canadian Imperial Bank of Commerce. Bertha, unfortunately, died shortly after their arrival in Victoria.

Laundy worked in the bank for a short period with Robert Service, and it was he who brought Service to the Cridge home to play tennis. Laundy became close to the bishop and Mary Cridge at the Church of Our Lord and was often invited to the Cridge home, where he met and fell in love with the bishop's daughter, Ellen. He married "Nell" at the Church of Our Lord early in 1891. As a wedding gift, Bishop Cridge provided them with a piece of land he no longer used, part of the Marifield estate. Their new home, named Glaslyn Cottage, was located on Simcoe Street, where all six of their children were born.

Richard, the Cridges' oldest son, who had been born at the parsonage in 1856 and survived the black measles epidemic, returned from Cambridge University, where he had obtained a degree in civil engineering. He, like Ellen, was provided with a piece of land from the Marifield estate and built a house on Simcoe Street where his wife and son lived. The house was known as Cridge Lodge. Richard travelled extensively as an engineer, building railways and worked on the E&N Railway on the Island. He married a teacher, Abigail Irene Polly from the United States, who was a United Empire Loyalist. While her husband travelled to faraway places to build railways, Abigail and her son relied on her mother- and father-in-law for advice and companionship. Richard was working in the Hawaiian Islands when he succumbed to a heart attack in September 1906. He had a known pulmonary condition, and his death was not a complete surprise.

Nevertheless, Abigail was badly shaken by her husband's death and in her sorrow relied heavily on the support of the Cridge family at Marifield. And so another generation began for Edward and Mary, who were involved with the upbringing of their grandson Edward, as was his delighted aunt Maude, who relished having a young boy around the house.

The passing years were not as kind to Bishop Hills as they were to Bishop Cridge. His stature and power were diminished by an 1879 decision of the Church of England authorities that created two dioceses in British Columbia. New Westminster, the larger of the two, included parishes on the mainland and in the interior, while Caledonia, Hills' diocese, was limited to only Vancouver Island and the Gulf Islands. Always grave, dignified, and somewhat aloof, he had never really become a part of his flock, nor been regarded fondly by the public. He met the early challenges of the colony, made substantial progress in advancing improvements in the fields of health and education, but he found the new settlement a difficult environment, one to which he did not adapt well.

He wrote in his early days that the people he encountered who were the least interested in religion were the miners, that he could find no rapport with them at all. Some people who knew him well thought he would have been better suited to a diocese in England, where his love of ritual and a more orderly lifestyle could have been satisfied. Perhaps he had thought the Pacific coast assignment was a stepping stone to grander things at home in England, but if so, this wish never materialized. As the years went by, and after his wife died in 1888, he lost his enthusiasm. After more than thirty years in British Columbia, he returned to England in 1892 and died at Parham vicarage in Suffolk in 1895, leaving no great mark on the history of British Columbia.

One of the major differences in the two men was that Hills remained an Englishman to the end, whereas Cridge became a Canadian pioneer of the West Coast. In addition, the Cridges raised a family and put down deep roots in Victoria, while Hills and his wife were childless and apart from the mainstream of the early residents.

Bishop Cridge watched sorrowfully the fate that befell another old antagonist, the man who had been his critic in the early years and then his supporter in the days and months following his clash with Bishop Hills, Amor De Cosmos. The eccentric, voluble, argumentative man who had rocketed to fame, even becoming the second premier of British Columbia, fell to earth just as quickly. He remained a Member of Parliament until his defeat in 1882, when he returned to Victoria from Ottawa, living in a house with his brother, Charles. Never married, De Cosmos began drinking heavily and acting even more strangely than he had in his younger years. He would walk up to people he met on the street and stare into their faces. He yelled one day at the coal baron Robert Dunsmuir, and this precipitated a bizarre duelling contest between the two elderly men, who brandished their canes at each other, fortunately without injury.[3]

Despite his erratic behaviour, De Cosmos could still sometimes be prescient, calling for nearby Swartz Bay to be developed as the main Victoria–Vancouver passenger boat terminal some sixty years before it happened. In 1895, he was found to be of unsound mind and a custodian was appointed to look after his financial affairs. De Cosmos had made his money in real estate, although there was an $87,000 mortgage on his $117,000 property investment in Chinatown. He died on July 4, 1897. The *Colonist*, the paper he had founded, stated that "he did the province much good service," although his passing was relatively unmarked elsewhere.[4]

The fact that his death was generally ignored brought a blistering letter to the editor from an old foe, Dr. Helmcken, who said it was a disgrace that there were only about sixty people at his funeral, and half that many at the graveside at Ross Bay. He wrote that this poor turnout made a mockery of a man who for forty years had been prominent in B.C. life and who had done much, not only for "fame, honor and glory." Dr. Helmcken chastised the community bitterly, saying that "governments, corporations and the public seem to have no heart, no sentiment, no memory — callous to all but their own interests or affairs."[5]

Bishop Cridge continued his church work, as did Mary, doing as much as possible to hold back the passing of the years. In 1887, the bishop addressed a large crowd in Beacon Hill Park celebrating the golden jubilee of Queen Victoria. He offered the opening prayer at the formal opening of the first session in the new legislative buildings, February 10, 1898, much as he had done at the very first meeting of the colony's governing assembly so long ago in the fort.

Mary and Edward Cridge, who had begun the first hospital in the colony, saw a dream fulfilled in 1890 when the spacious Royal Jubilee Hospital was opened. With his great shock of hair and flowing white beard, Edward was a familiar, well-recognized figure on the streets of Victoria as he and Mary made their daily rounds. Another significant event heralded more modernization for Victoria, but it also brought feelings of nostalgia for the Cridge family. Demolition of Fort Victoria was complete by 1864. This was the structure Douglas had begun in 1843 and had been Edward and Mary's first home on Vancouver Island. It had been a fort in name only. Its walls had never been assailed and its canons never fired in defence, but for many years it had been the heart of the small settlement. The demolition crew was amazed at the workmanship they found in the fort, which had been built by men with little training, using only the most basic of tools. The builders had often improvised, but the construction was all carefully done and the finishing was impressive. The auctioneer P. M. Backus sold the land for redevelopment. A prime lot, fifty feet on Government Street and seventy on Fort Street, went for $11,500 to A. Munro, "after considerable competition."[6] Most of the lots sold for between $3,000 and $4,000 and the fort was soon replaced by new buildings, leaving not a trace of it behind — only its place in history. In 1895, Bishop Cridge was granted an honorary degree by the Presbyterian College in Montreal for his contribution to religion. At the turn of the century, he was chosen to give a blessing for Victoria men who marched away to fight the Boers in South Africa.

During his last year as rector of the Church of Our Lord, the elderly Edward, usually accompanied by Mary, attended many public events. The highlight of the year for them in 1901 was the visit to Victoria by their

Royal Highnesses the Duke and Duchess of Cornwall and York, who arrived aboard the RMS *Empress of India* on October 1. At the Mount Baker Hotel, which had been totally refurbished for the event, the provincial government hosted a reception and dinner for Prince Albert and the duchess, who would later become King George VI and Queen Mary. At the lavish affair held in the royals' honour, Edward was seated next to the duchess while Mary was beside the Duke. Mary had been escorted into the dinner by a naval admiral and was deep in conversation with him for the early part of the meal. Then she turned her attention to the gentleman on her left and held a lengthy conversation with the man, unaware of who he was. He said he had been married for eight years and that he and his wife had three children. In the course of their conversation she remarked, "We Victorians have been very excited about the royal visit and have rather stood in awe of entertaining royalty."

"And why," he asked, "is it because you are afraid of talking to them?"

"Yes," Mary replied, "I suppose so."

"Well," he said, "you are talking very nicely to me. Why should you not talk the same to them?"

"Oh," she said, "that is different."

Their conversation ranged over several topics, including the future of his children with careers in the navy and the extensive travel he must undertake, but not once did Mary realize who he was. After the meal he took her to meet his wife, who had been Edward's companion during dinner. They had been seated on the same side of the table and not visible to each other. Mary blushed, immediately admitted her mistake, and apologized to the duchess for not recognizing her husband. The duchess laughed, "Oh, that is just what he likes, that is the sort of thing he enjoys." The following day the Cridges received personally signed photographs of the duke and duchess with their children. Mary related her experiences to Maude as soon as she returned home and so the story became part of the family history.[7]

In 1902, Bishop Cridge reluctantly resigned as rector of the Church of

Edward and Mary Cridge, Golden wedding anniversary, 1904
(CHURCH OF OUR LORD ARCHIVES)

Our Lord. The congregation knew he was an old man, and his departure was to be expected, but still they could not imagine life without the preacher they loved so well and had followed from the very beginning. They gave him a leather purse containing cash to mark his eightieth birthday.

In his retirement, he kept a close eye on current affairs, particularly anything to do with his old bogey, religious ritualism. His papers in Victoria's provincial archives, in addition to many copies of his sermons laboriously written out by hand, contain some old newspaper clippings. One warns of ritual "tyranny" in Quebec; another that he must have been particularly fond of cites a Member of Parliament for Liverpool who proposed a bill in the House of Commons making illegal any and all trappings of the

Catholic faith in the Church of England. It did not pass, probably much to the bishop's disappointment.

Bishop Cridge was always conscious of history, and in retirement he sent a message to the Church of Our Lord congregation reminding them of "those brave and noble men and women, rich and poor, young and old, who came out in a body because they could not bear to have their worship tainted with error."[8]

24

A Legacy of Social Reform

After a partnership that had lasted fifty years, Mary Cridge died in December 1905, widely mourned by all who had known her. She was recognized for her great love of her community and her family, her significant social contributions to early Victoria life, and her courage in the face of tragedy and the unknown. Her determination and untiring efforts on behalf of all those who needed help had personally affected many of those who mourned her passing. None mourned more than Edward, who dedicated a new lectern in the Church of Our Lord to "Mary Beloved Wife of Rt. Rev. Bishop Cridge, D.D. 19 December, 1905."

As he had confided in his diary so long ago, Edward Cridge's love for Mary had led him to marriage, overcoming earlier fears that it would interfere with his work. She had become not an obstacle to his work but his inspiration. She had been his helpmate in pushing for social advancement and creating health facilities and welfare opportunities for the people of Victoria; she had shared his deep religious beliefs, which helped them overcome tragedy and loss. Mary Cridge was an imaginative, sensitive and inquiring woman who had moved a long way from the quiet of rural England to create a full and satisfying life in a new but well-loved land. She was buried in Ross Bay Cemetery.

In December of 1908, three years after his wife's death, Edward celebrated his ninetieth birthday, with dozens of people coming to Marifield to wish him well. He was bright and cheerful, sitting in his big chair by the fireplace to greet family, parishioners, friends, and government and civic officials. In all, some four hundred people expressed their birthday wishes. When he was presented with a purse containing two hundred and one dollars in gold coins, he was slightly overcome, stating that the members of council and his friends were "far kinder than I merited." The attendees murmured their disagreement. Civic officials read a special proclamation passed by the council to honour his birthday. It praised his many contributions, which had been vital to the progress of the city, stating that in his long lifetime he had been "a man of proud views, full of benevolence and energy." It added that he was held in great respect and esteem "by all classes of the community for his charitable spirit and many good works."[1]

The bishop in his acknowledgement to the guests at his home did not hesitate to mention that his wife Mary had played an equal role in their life's work. He noted that when he first met her in England he knew she was the one the Lord had appointed to be his wife. Mary had laboured faithfully in building their church and had been a major figure in the creation of the hospital and the orphanage. As he wrote later, "She was to me better than any curate in her relations to the congregation. I bless my Lord who made her all this to me and more in over 50 years."[2] He smiled as those gathered in his honour sang, "Happy Birthday" to the old, much-loved man.

Despite the loss of his partner, the loss of his only remaining son, Richard, in Honolulu and his failing health, Bishop Cridge remained sharp-minded and feisty, sending a letter to the *Colonist* in 1912 pointing out that in a story about him they had called him a missionary — many of whom were not ordained — whereas he had been a minister before he came to Victoria. Toward the end of his life he loved to sit in the garden at Marifield and sing hymns with his family. On May 6, 1913, his long life came to an end. One of the last to visit him at home was an old Chinese gentleman who had worked for the family for years.

In a final, gentle gesture, his daughters, sons-in-law and grandchildren stood around the old man's bed and sang his favourite hymn, "The Head That Once Was Crowned with Thorns." He died as dawn was breaking on a beautiful spring day, the scent of the trees and flowers filtering into his room, many of them developed from seeds he had brought and nurtured from his native England so many eventful years before.

The Cridges were survived by three daughters out of their original family of nine children. The two older girls had married to become Mary Cran and Ellen Laundy, and Maude, the youngest, remained at home and cared for her parents into their old age as well as her young nephew, Richard's son Edward.

The bishop's passing was greatly mourned in Victoria, where he received glowing tributes and fitting accolades. Among its comments, the *Colonist* noted shortly before his death that "in his long lifetime he has tried to make every one he knew happier and better." As news of his passing spread, flags flew at half-mast all over the city, including at the legislature, Christ Church Cathedral, the Union Club and many commercial buildings. Leading figures from all walks of life in the capital filled the pews along with the congregation and overflowed into the grounds. Bells pealed on the day of the bishop's funeral, and the *Colonist* wrote that it was one of the biggest funerals in the city for many years. Over one hundred floral tributes adorned the church.

Charles Hayward, one of the pallbearers, had the honour of being the oldest friend of the late bishop, having attended his church and Sunday

*Funeral of Bishop Edward Cridge at the Church of Our Lord,
Victoria, May 9, 1913* (BC ARCHIVES, A-01207)

school as a boy in England. Hayward's father had been a church warden at Christ Church in West Ham, and Cridge's letters describing Victoria had induced the Haywards to make the voyage to the colony fifty years earlier. Charles Hayward had known the bishop for fifty-five years.

In his quiet way, the bishop would have found one notation mildly amusing. The words under the picture of his funeral in the *Colonist* said he was being carried out of Christ Church Cathedral. No, that was the church he had walked out of almost forty years earlier. He was being carried from his own Church of Our Lord. He was buried at Ross Bay Cemetery beside his beloved Mary.

After the death of Bishop Cridge in 1913 and the demise of many of his elderly friends and original parishioners, the congregation at the Church of

Our Lord declined somewhat. Cridge was succeeded by his assistant, the Reverend Dr. John Reid, then by the Rev. Thomas Gladstone, Rev. Arthur Owen and Rev. George Scarrett. Cridge's son-in-law Thomas Laundy then filled in when he retired from the bank. Laundy became first a deacon at the Church of Our Lord and then an ordained minister at the ripe old age of eighty-six. He served from 1944 to 1951. At the time, the *Colonist* reported, "Mr. Laundy, at 86, is rector emeritus of the Church of Our Lord. He is the oldest parishioner, too." He remained the minister until he was succeeded by the Rev. J.G. Brown in 1952.

Many years later, on July 5, 1998, Cridge's church was recognized by the government of Canada as a National Historic Site. Sophia Leung, MP for Vancouver-Kingsway, paid tribute to the part the little church had played in the growth of the community for more than a hundred years. "These are places we visit to rejuvenate our souls and to learn more about ourselves and our past. Historic sites such as the Church of Our Lord are a source of pride for Canadians as well as symbols of Canada," said the MP at a ceremony marking the installation of a commemorative plaque at the church entrance.[3] Much interior and exterior restoration work was done in 1999 in a project to mark the church's 125th anniversary. It included completion of a hall begun in 1929, work that had been constantly postponed because of funding problems. The Church of Our Lord remains a city landmark, almost in the shadow of the Empress Hotel and new high-rise apartment buildings. It is close to the harbour where the Cridges first saw Fort Victoria and met James Douglas.

Inside the church are records of the past and, in particular, a sacred book commemorating a date of great significance. Sitting on a table is a big black Bible showing the wear of time and travel. It is inscribed, "To Edward and Mary Cridge on their marriage with earnest wishes for their temporal and spiritual happenings from their affectionate friend and brother, J. Lambert Knowles, Sept. 14, 1854."

The Church of Our Lord remains a vigorous institution in the heart of Victoria, but the Reformed Episcopal movement did not spread widely throughout North America. Besides the Church of Our Lord, there are only two other congregations in British Columbia and four in the rest of Canada, all in Ontario.[4] There are approximately one hundred and fifty parishes in the United States.

* * *

The name Cridge lives on in the province in many ways — from the modern, busy social centre in Victoria to lonely northern peaks and Pacific coastal waters. South of Prince Rupert lies Cridge Island, named in honour of Edward Cridge in 1862 by the crew of HMS *Hecate*. Cridge Passage, between Farrant and Fin Island, off Banks Island, was named in 1866 by Captain Daniel Pender of the Royal Navy. During an earlier voyage in 1865, Captain Pender, whose name was given to two of the Gulf Islands, North Pender and South Pender, also named a mountain after Cridge as well as the main creek that runs down its slopes. Another nearby peak and a creek he named Mount Hills and Hills Creek, the only place names associated with the first Church of England bishop in British Columbia. Both mountains are west of Knight Inlet, east of the Ahunhatic River, and there is another Cridge Peak west of Butedale.

Yet the legacy of Edward and Mary Cridge lives on not just in place names but in social achievements that are now cornerstones of modern society. In their final years the quiet reformers could watch with joy the development of the hospital and the orphanage in which they had played founding roles. The pair had been advocates of a wide spectrum of social reform issues. These ranged from overseeing the development of the school system to women's rights to jail reform and support for immigration, which included encouraging the Church to sponsor "bride ships." The democratic freedom they had envisaged for the colony was firmly entrenched. Beyond all that, their spiritual sense of commitment to their fellow human beings influenced the many people with whom they came in contact, and that influence continues into the present day.

The noted Canadian Anglican historian, Frank A. Peake, looking at the early Anglican church on the Pacific coast, quotes a small verse that is a tribute to Christian believers like Edward and Mary Cridge and others who ventured onto the distant Pacific coast so many years ago:

> They climbed the steep ascent to heaven,
> Through peril, work and pain,
> O God to us may grace be given,
> To follow in their train.[5]

Chronology

1817   DECEMBER 17: Edward Cridge is born in the small village of Bratton-Flemming in Devonshire, southwest England, the son of John and Grace Dyer Cridge.

1827   APRIL 15: Mary Winmill is born in at Dagenham, Essex, to Mr. and Mrs. George Winmill.

1846   The British and American governments sign the Oregon Treaty, setting the forty-ninth parallel as the international boundary west of the Rocky Mountains, and James Douglas is appointed Hudson's Bay Company agent for all of Vancouver Island.

1848   After graduating from Cambridge and teaching grammar school at Walsham, Norfolk, Edward is ordained a Church of England deacon at Norwich Cathedral.

1851   Edward is appointed curate at Christ Church, West Ham, near London, where he meets Mary Winmill, a schoolteacher at the church.

OCTOBER 31: James Douglas becomes governor of Vancouver Island but also maintains his role as chief factor for the Hudson's Bay Company.

1854   SEPTEMBER: Edward marries Mary Winmill and they leave England for Fort Victoria, along with three family retainers.

1855   APRIL 1: The Reverend Edward and Mary Cridge step ashore at Fort Victoria after a journey of more than six months aboard the *Marquis of Bute*.

DECEMBER 18: Edward's sisters Elizabeth and Mary arrive in Fort Victoria aboard the *Princess Royal*, to assist with teaching at the soon-to-be-established parsonage school.

1856   JUNE: Richard Coombe Cridge is born, Edward and Mary Cridges' first child.

JULY 22: First election is held on Vancouver Island, followed by the first session of the House of Assembly in a room at Fort Victoria on August 12.

AUGUST 31: First service takes place in the first Protestant church built near Fort Victoria, which the Reverend Cridge names Christ Church.

1857   OCTOBER: Edward Scott Cridge is born, a second son for Edward and Mary.

1858   APRIL 25: The American steamer the *Commodore* arrives in Victoria harbour from San Francisco with hundreds of gold miners aboard, the first in a large wave.

AUGUST: The mainland officially becomes the Crown colony of British Columbia.

AUGUST: The Reverend James Gammage arrives in Fort Victoria to serve as a roving missionary for the Church of England.

DECEMBER: A cottage at Yates and Broad streets is rented as Victoria's first hospital, possibly the only one north of San Francisco.

DECEMBER 11: Amor De Cosmos launches his four-page *Weekly British Colonist*, destined to become Victoria's first regular newspaper.

DECEMBER 25: The Reverend William Burton Crickmer arrives with his family to minister to a second Church of England congregation in the colony.

1860   JANUARY: Bishop George Hills, the first Church of England bishop of the newly created diocese of Columbia, arrives in Victoria.

AUGUST: Mary Hills Cridge is born, the couple's first daughter, named after her mother and the bishop who christens her in September.

SEPTEMBER: The Reverend Cridge is officially designated rector of Christ Church, Victoria, by the newly arrived Bishop Hills, although he had been acting minister there since 1856.

1861   James Douglas declares Victoria a city.

1862   MARCH: Twins Grace and Eber join the Cridge household, their second daughter and third son, respectively.

SEPTEMBER: The "bride ship" *Tynemouth* arrives in Victoria with sixty-two unmarried women aboard, sponsored by the Church of England to work as domestics in the colony.

1864   FEBRUARY: A sixth child and fourth son, Frederick Pemberton Cridge, is born to Edward and Mary.

FEBRUARY: Edward is elevated from rector to dean of Christ Church by Bishop Hills.

James Douglas retires as governor of the colony of British Columbia, replaced by Captain Arthur Edward Kennedy.

1864–65   Black measles claim the lives of four of the Cridge children between December and March: Frederick, ten months; Edward, seven; and the twins Grace and Eber, almost three.

1865   JULY 13: Mary gives birth to another daughter, Rhoda, who suffers ill health from the start. She dies at the tender age of twenty-one, in 1886.

AUGUST: Alfred Waddington replaces Edward Cridge as the first full-time, paid superintendent of education in the colony but resigns within a year.

1866   JULY 30: A telegraph line is completed to Victoria, linking the city to the world beyond.

NOVEMBER 19: Vancouver Island and the mainland colony are united and named British Columbia with its capital in Victoria.

1867   MARCH 18: Ellen Cridge is born to Edward and Mary at Sellindge Cottage.

JULY 1: The four eastern provinces of Ontario, Quebec, Nova Scotia and New Brunswick unite to form Canada.

1868   AUGUST 20: Maude enters the world at Sellindge Cottage, Edward and Mary's ninth and last child.

1869	OCTOBER 1: A mysterious fire destroys Christ Church in Victoria.
1870	Governor Frederick Seymour dies suddenly and is replaced by Anthony Musgrave, who pushes British Columbia to enter Confederation.
1871	JULY 1: British Columbia joins Canadian Confederation, the sixth province to do so.
1872	NOVEMBER: Church ladies establish an orphanage in a small house; it moves to larger premises by 1873 and becomes known as the B.C. Protestant Orphans' Home. A hundred-bed home is built by 1891 on Hillside Avenue.
	DECEMBER 5: An evening sermon delivered by Archdeacon William Reece of the mainland as part of celebrations to consecrate the new Christ Church Cathedral sparks a religious controversy for Dean Cridge, Bishop Hills and the Church of England in Victoria.
1874	SEPTEMBER 10: Dean Cridge, summoned by Bishop Hills, appears before an ecclesiastical court convened at the Pandora Street hall and eight days later is suspended as dean of Christ Church.
	SEPTEMBER 24: Dean Cridge is legally forbidden to enter Christ Church Cathedral, in a decision handed down by Supreme Court Judge Matthew Begbie.
	OCTOBER 29: Cridge announces to a packed meeting at the Pandora Street hall his intention to join the recently formed Reformed Episcopal Church and to establish a new evangelical church in Victoria.
1875	The Cridge family moves into Marifield, next door to the Richard Carr family, after Edward and Mary's dream home is completed on the old Beckley Farm estate.
1876	JANUARY 16: Cridge conducts the first service in the newly completed Church of Our Lord, built for a total cost of twelve thousand dollars.
1877	AUGUST 2: The "Father of British Columbia" James Douglas dies in Victoria, age seventy-four. His funeral cortege on August 7 is the longest ever seen in the city.
1880	The Cridges' eldest daughter, Mary, marries Victoria banker James Cran at the Church of Our Lord.
1890	Royal Jubilee Hospital opens in Victoria, a dream fulfilled for the Cridges, who had established the city's first hospital in 1858
1891	Ellen or "Nell," the Cridges' fourth daughter (second-eldest daughter of the three remaining), marries the banker Thomas Herbert Laundy.

1892   Bishop George Hills, a widower, returns to England and dies there in
        1895, little remembered in British Columbia where he was the first
        Anglican bishop.

1897   Amor De Cosmos, the founder of Victoria's first regular newspaper
        and British Columbia's second premier, dies.

1902   Bishop Cridge retires as rector of the Church of Our Lord.

1905   DECEMBER 19: Edward's beloved wife Mary Cridge dies, in her seventy-
        ninth year.

1906   SEPTEMBER: The Cridges' eldest child and sole remaining son, Richard,
        dies of a heart attack while working in the Hawaiian Islands, leaving his
        wife Abigail and son Edward.

1908   DECEMBER 17: Dozens congregate at Marifield to celebrate Bishop
        Cridge's ninetieth birthday, and he receives more than four hundred
        birthday wishes.

1913   MAY 6: Bishop Edward Cridge dies at home at Marifield, in his
        ninety-sixth year.

Notes

1 / EDWARD AND MARY (pp. 5–14)

1 Testimonial from John Shillibeer, headmaster of Oundle Grammar School, quoted in Robert G. Dennison, "A Leap of Faith: The Early Years of the Reverend Edward Cridge," *British Columbia History* (Journal of the British Columbia Historical Federation) 39, no. 1 (2006): 4, http://bchistory.ca/publications/journal/oldjournals/39.1_2006.pdf (accessed April 10, 2010).

2 Edward Cridge, diary, Edward Cridge fonds, MS-0320; MS-0420, BC Archives, Victoria, B.C. (hereafter cited as Edward Cridge diary). To avoid excessive citation, if this source is identified in the text, it is not footnoted.

3 Bishop Edward Cridge, *As It Was in the Beginning* (Chicago, 1890). This book by Cridge explained his views on life in general and the role of the Church in relation to freedom of the individual.

4 The couple's wedding presents are listed in an essay by Edgar Fawcett, "Reminiscences of Bishop Cridge" [published in the *Colonist* in 1913], Church of Our Lord Archives, Victoria, B.C.

1 Mary Cridge, letter, MS-1975, photocopy [1855], 1944, BC Archives, Victoria, B.C. This "letter" is a typewritten document, transcribed by a relative, with copies preserved in the BC Archives and City of Victoria Archives. The original is in the Church of Our Lord archives. Subsequent quotes in this chapter are from the same source, unless otherwise cited in the text.

1 Quoted by Margaret A. Ormsby, "Douglas, Sir James," *The Canadian Encyclopedia* (Toronto: McClelland & Stewart, 1990), 683, http://www.thecanadianencyclopedia.com/index.cfm?PgNm=TCE&Params=A1ARTA0002373 (accessed April 10, 2010).

2 Margaret A. Ormsby, "Douglas, Sir James," *Dictionary of Canadian Biography Online*, vol. 10, *1871–1880* (University of Toronto/Université Laval, 2000), http://www.biographi.ca/009004-119.01-e.php?&id_nbr=4955&interval=20&&PHPSESSID=uiggt850s17c17orv46ukap3g4 (accessed April 10, 2010).

3 Margaret A. Ormsby, *British Columbia: A History* (Vancouver: Macmillan Company of Canada, 1958), 80, on which the following discussion of the building of Fort Victoria relies.

1 Edward Cridge diary.

2 Douglas and his wife had five daughters when they moved into the fort but one of the children died very shortly thereafter. Two more were born at Fort Victoria in the years that followed, and their home was always the centre of social activity in the community. In total they had thirteen children, but a number died at birth or in their early years. Only four outlived them. Clearly Douglas wanted education for his own children, but he also needed a Church of England school to please the British government and encourage immigration from Britain.

3 Ormsby, *British Columbia*, 104.

4 Robert John Staines to Edward Cridge, 26 October 1849, Edward Cridge fonds, BC Archives. Also Ormsby, *British Columbia*, 119.

1 John Sebastian Helmcken, *Reminiscences of John Sebastian Helmcken*, ed. Dorothy B. Smith (Vancouver: UBC Press, in co-operation with the Provincial Archives of British Columbia, 1975). The Reverend Staines, in comparison, had annoyed Douglas when he refused to eat in the mess hall and so was not in attendance to say grace for the men employed by the Hudson's Bay Company.

2 Helmcken, *Reminiscences*, 147.

3 Ibid., 120.

4 Information about Macdonald is based on discussions with Sylvia Van Kirk, Church of Our Lord Archives, Victoria, B.C.; plus Reformed Episcopal Church (Anglican), Diocese of Western Canada & Alaska and the Mission District of Cuba, "The History and Founding Principles of the Reformed Episcopal Church" (Victoria, B.C., 2009), http://www.recwcan.ca/history.htm (accessed May 17, 2010).

5 Edward Cridge fonds, MS-0320; MS-0420, BC Archives.

6 Ibid.

7 Helmcken, *Reminiscences*, 333.

8 *British Weekly Colonist* (Victoria, B.C.), n.d.

9 Mary Cridge memo to herself.

6 / THE END OF COMPANY RULE (pp. 44–51)

1 The charter had been signed on January 13, 1849. It granted the Hudson's Bay Company control of all Vancouver Island for ten years, with the proviso that within five years a settlement of colonists be established. If no settlement came into being, the Island would revert to the Crown on May 30, 1859. The Crown could also repurchase the colony with compensation to the Hudson's Bay Company for its establishment and properties at any time in the interim. This is what it chose to do on August 20, 1858. Records relating to the lease and sale of land on Vancouver Island, HBCQAB.226/Z/1 fos. 45–59d, Hudson's Bay Company Archives, University of Manitoba, Winnipeg.

2 This first governing body was ineffective, as quickly became obvious. It was a council rather than a designated legislative body, which came later, in 1856.

3 Quoted by Ormsby, *British Columbia*, 122.

4 *British Weekly Colonist*, n.d.

5 Helmcken statement from *Victoria Colonist*, n.d.; also mentioned in Reginald Eyre Watters, ed., *British Columbia: A Centennial Anthology* (Toronto: McClelland & Stewart, 1958).

6 Helmcken, *Reminiscences*, 329.

7 *British Weekly Colonist*, n.d.

8 Ormsby, "Douglas, Sir James," *Dictionary of Canadian Biography Online*.

7 / EDUCATION IN THE COLONY (pp. 52–57)

1 *British Colonist*, October 10, 1859.

2 Information on Demers throughout the story is gleaned from the *Colonist* newspaper and Douglas biographies by Ormsby.

3 Record of proceedings August 12, 1856, House of Assembly, Legislative Archives, Victoria, B.C. This was the date of the first meeting of the legislative committee that had been elected in June; Edward's report on the schools was given November 30, 1856.

4 Ibid.

5 Quotes in this and next three paragraphs are from the Edward Cridge fonds, MS-0320; MS-0420, BC Archives.

6 Edward Cridge diary. Mary's sickness was long and often painful, in an era before easy diagnosis and successful treatment of TB, and after being bedridden for more than ten years, she died in 1870 at fifty years of age. "Tuberculosis was the deadliest disease of the nineteenth and early twentieth century in the Western world" according to Allison Kirk-Montgomery and Shelley McKellar, *Medicine and Technology in Canada, 1900–1950*, Transformation Series 16 (Ottawa: Canada Science and Technology Museum, 2008), 43. The authors report that the "bacillus tuberculosis" was discovered in 1882, before which the disease was, based on its "wasting" symptoms, called consumption, phthisis or the "white plague."

7 *British Weekly Colonist*, January 1, 1859.

8 Ibid., April 16, 1859.

9 *British Colonist*, July 12, 1860.

8 / GOLD! MINERS RUSH IN (pp. 58–64)

1 *Victoria Gazette*, n.d.

2 Edward Cridge diary.

3 *British Weekly Colonist*, n.d.

4 Edward Cridge fonds, MS-0320; MS-0420, BC Archives, Victoria, B.C. This quote and the next one are from Cridge's Sunday sermons and also appeared also in the *Colonist* newspaper.

5 *British Weekly Colonist*, February 5, 1859.

9 / A HOSPITAL FOR VICTORIA (pp. 65–68)

1 *British Weekly Colonist*, December 18, 1858.

2 Edward Cridge fonds, and newspaper clippings, BC Archives. Much of this information came from notes provided by David Laundy and from Fawcett, "Reminiscences of Bishop Cridge" (see note 4). Fawcett met Cridge when he was twelve years old and knew him for fifty-four years.

3 Legislative report by Cridge, as clerk of the House of Assembly. He also made notes for himself, which are in the BC Archives, and the issue was picked up by the *Colonist* for public discussion.

4 *Daily British Colonist*, March 25, 1862.

5 *British Colonist*, n.d.

6 Edward Cridge diary.

1 The Colonial Church and School Society was apparently a unit under the Society for the Propagation of the Gospel, which was responsible for just about everything in the colonies. Their annual reports are available through Library and Archives Canada.

2 George Hills, *No Better Land: The 1860 Diaries of the Anglican Colonial Bishop George Hills*, ed. Roberta L. Bagshaw (Victoria: Sono Nis Press, 1996).

3 George Woodcock, *Amor De Cosmos: Journalist and Reformer* (Toronto: Oxford University Press, 1975).

4 When the city's two dailies, the other being the *Victoria Times*, amalgamated in the 1980s as the *Times Colonist*, some old-timers felt the paper should have been called the *Colonist Times* because the *Colonist* was the older of the two.

5 *British Colonist*, July 5, 1860.

6 There was little else to read until Victoria's first public library opened late in 1861. It operated on a $5 membership and a $1 monthly fee, alleviating to a considerable extent the shortage of reading material. *Colonist*, n.d.

1 "The very model of an Anglican prelate" is quoted in "Hills, George," ABC-BookWorld [website], first line, http://www.abcbookworld.com/view_author.php?id=4995 (accessed June 4, 2010). The biography of George Hills is based on information from George A. Hills, *A Tour in British Columbia* (London: Clay Printers, 1861), and Hills, *No Better Land*.

2 Edward Cridge diary.

3 Bishop George Hills, diary, 1860, BC Archives, plus subsequent quotes.

4 Quoted by Ormsby, "Douglas, Sir James," *Dictionary of Canadian Biography Online*.

5 *British Colonist*, December 3, 1859.

6 Ibid., n.d.

7 *Daily British Colonist*, August 28, 1860.

8 Vernon Story, et al., *The Home: Orphans' Home to Family Center, 1873–1998* (Victoria: Cridge Center for the Family, 1999), 28.

1 *Daily British Colonist*, October 11–13, 1860, plus subsequent quotes from Hills' report.

2 Ibid., October 24, 1860.

3 Ibid.

4 Ibid., January 31, 1861.

5 Ibid., February 18, 1861.

6 Ibid., March 14, 1861.

7 Ibid., March 26, 1861.

13 / DEPARTURES AND ARRIVALS (pp. 93–97)

1 *Daily British Colonist*, June 12, 1862.
2 Ibid., June 16, 1862.
3 Ibid., March 26, 1862.
4 Ibid., September 19, 1862.
5 Ibid., September 20, 1862.
6 Ibid., September 29, 1862.
7 Ibid., September 22, 1862.
8 Daryl Ashby, *John Muir: West Coast Pioneer* (Vancouver: Ronsdale Press, 2005).

14 / VICTORIA — A CITY OF ALMOST SIX THOUSAND (pp. 98–103)

1 *Daily British Colonist*, February 6, 1862.
2 *Victoria Directory*, Howard & Barnett, Victoria, 1863.
3 *Daily British Colonist*, May 5, 1863.
4 Ibid., February 21, 1863.
5 Fawcett, "Reminiscences."
6 This society was established in 1804 to distribute bibles in Wales.
7 Mary Cridge to Edward Cridge, Edward Cridge fonds, MS-0320, BC Archives.
8 For a full account of Duncan's missionary activities, see Susan Neylan, *The Heavens Are Changing* (Montreal: McGill-Queen's University Press, 2003).
9 *Daily British Colonist*, 1864.

15 / DOUGLAS RETIRES FROM OFFICE (pp. 104–109)

1 Ormsby, "Douglas, Sir James," *Dictionary of Canadian Biography Online*.
2 *Daily British Colonist*, May 1864.
3 Ibid., April 4, 1864.
4 Ibid., April 11, 1864, and subsequent quotes. Information about Waddington also relies on the authors' previous book, Betty O'Keefe and Ian Macdonald, *Disaster on Mount Slesse: The Story of Western Canada's Worst Air Crash* (Madeira Park, B.C.: Caitlin Press, 2006).
5 *Daily British Colonist*, May 13, 1864.
6 Ibid., June 2, 1864.
7 Ibid., November 7, 1864.

16 / TRAGEDY AT HOME (pp. 110–114)

1 Fawcett, "Reminiscences."
2 Quoted by Ashby, *John Muir*, 202.

17 / POLITICAL CHANGES AND A SUSPICIOUS FIRE (pp. 115–120)

1 *Daily British Colonist*, October, 1865.
2 Ibid., July 31, 1866.

18 / MARY'S ORPHANAGE (pp. 121–124)

1 Vernon Story, et al., *The Home: Orphans' Home to Family Center, 1873–1998* (Victoria: Cridge Center for the Family, 1999).

2 The volunteer board of directors included, in 2010, Greg Cran, great-great-grandson of the Cridges' daughter Mary, as president, and Michael Cridge, a descendant of their oldest son Richard, as treasurer.

19 / TROUBLES BREW IN THE CATHEDRAL (pp. 125–134)

1 Edward Cridge fonds, MS-0320; MS-0420, BC Archives.

2 Bishop George Hills, diary, BC Archives.

3 *Daily British Colonist*, December 6, 1872, plus information about the service and its aftermath.

4 Ibid., December 8, 1872.

5 Ibid., December 24, 1872.

6 Ibid., September 11, 1874.

20 / THE REFORMED EPISCOPAL CHURCH (pp. 135–139)

1 *Daily British Colonist*, September 16, 1874.

2 Ibid., September 18, 1874. ·

3 Ibid.

4 Ibid., September 19, 1874.

5 Ibid., September 29, 1874.

6 Ibid., October 13, 1874.

21 / A NEW CHURCH IS BORN (pp. 140–147)

1 Edward Cridge fonds, MS-0320; MS-0420, BC Archives.

2 Emily Carr, *The Book of Small* (Toronto, Vancouver: Clarke, Irwin & Co., 1966), 112.

3 *Daily British Colonist*, January 18, 1876.

4 The Heritage Co-ordinator of the Church of Our Lord, Sylvia Van Kirk, notes that the Free Church of England still exists although it is not very strong today. The American Church is quite well established, especially in the south. In 2008, the Church of Our Lord was host to the General Council of the Reformed Episcopal Church and several hundred delegates came from all over the states. The Reformed Episcopal Church is now under the umbrella of the Anglican Church of North America.

22 / MARIFIELD AND EMILY CARR (pp. 148–155)

1 Heeley's was one of many tributes made following Cridge's death and carried in the *Colonist*. Edward Cridge fonds, MS-0320; MS-0420, BC Archives.

2 Emily Carr, *The Book of Small* (Toronto, Vancouver: Clarke, Irwin & Co., 1966).

3 Ibid., 27.

4 Ibid., 24.

5 Ibid., 7.

23 / THE PASSING OF THREE PIONEERS (pp. 156–165)

1 Edward Cridge diary.

2 James Douglas's funeral was reported in the *Colonist*, which is the source for this account, including the quotes from Archdeacon Wright. A copy of Bishop Cridge's sermon is in the Edward Cridge fonds, MS-0320, BC Archives.

3 *Daily Colonist*, n.d.

4 Ibid., July 6, 1897.

5 Ibid., July 9, 1897.

6 Ibid., n.d.

7 David Laundy, personal communication, Victoria, B.C.

8 Edward Cridge fonds, MS-0320; MS-0420, BC Archives.

24 / A LEGACY OF SOCIAL REFORM (pp. 166–172)

1 *Daily Colonist*, December 1908.

2 Edward Cridge fonds, MS-0320; MS-0420, BC Archives.

3 *Times Colonist* (Victoria, B.C.), July 1998.

4 In Ontario: Trinity Reformed Episcopal Church Cathedral, New Liskeard; Saint Augustine's Reformed Episcopal Church, Toronto; Grace Chapel, Gowganda; The Church of the Good Shepherd, South Orillia. In the Diocese of Western Canada and Alaska: The Church of Our Lord, Victoria; Living Word Episcopal Church, Courtenay; Church of the Holy Trinity, Colwood.

5 Frank A. Peake, *The Anglican Church in British Columbia* (Vancouver: Mitchell Press, 1959), 119-20.

Bibliography

Research for this biography was based largely on primary sources, including documents in private and public collections. Much of the information comes from handwritten notes and envelopes, family comments, and interviews with relevant sources, or it was culled from historical biographies. We have tried to document important sources. This bibliography includes some general references not cited directly in the notes.

The text also relies to a great extent on early issues of local newspapers, for which specific dates and page numbers were not always available. Among the Victoria newspapers consulted were the *Evening Telegram*, the *Gazette*, the *Daily Times*, and the *Daily Colonist* in various editions, plus the *Times Colonist* 2008 anniversary edition. The *British Weekly Colonist* was the original name of the paper, which later became the *British Colonist* and the *Daily Colonist*.

PRIMARY SOURCES

Cridge, Edward. Edward Cridge fonds, MS-0320; MS-0420. BC Archives, Victoria, B.C.

Fawcett, Edgar. "Reminiscences of Bishop Cridge" [essay published in the *Colonist* in 1913]. Church of Our Lord Archives, Victoria, B.C.

Hills, Bishop George. Diaries. BC Archives, Victoria, B.C.

"History of the Church of Our Lord" [booklet]. Revised 2009. Church of Our Lord Archives, Victoria, B.C.

Record of proceedings August 12, 1856. House of Assembly. Legislative Archives, Victoria, B.C.

Records relating to the lease and sale of land on Vancouver Island. HBCQAB.226/Z/1 fos. 45–59d. Hudson's Bay Company Archives, University of Manitoba, Winnipeg.

Victoria Directory, 1860, 1863 (Howard & Barnett). BC Archives, Victoria, B.C.

SECONDARY SOURCES

Akrigg, G.P.V., and Helen B. Akrigg. *British Columbia Place Names*. Vancouver: UBC Press, 1997.

Ashby, Daryl. *John Muir: West Coast Pioneer*. Vancouver: Ronsdale Press, 2005.

Barman, Jean. *The West Beyond the West: A History of British Columbia*. Toronto: University of Toronto Press, 1991.

Carr, Emily. *The Book of Small*. Vancouver: Douglas & McIntyre, 2004.

Cridge, Bishop Edward. *As It Was in the Beginning*. Chicago, 1890.

Dennison, Robert G. "A Leap of Faith: The Early Years of the Reverend Edward Cridge." *British Columbia History* (Journal of the British Columbia Historical Federation) 39, no. 1 (2006): 4–9. http://bchistory.ca/publications/journal/oldjournals/39.1_2006.pdf (accessed April 10, 2010).

———. "Cridge: The Making of a Bishop." *British Columbia History*, 40, no. 3 (2007): 2–7. http://bchistory.ca/publications/journal/oldjournals/40.3_2007.pdf (accessed April 10, 2010).

Dickinson, Susan. "Edward Cridge and George Hills: Doctrinal Conflict, 1872–1874, and the Founding of Church of Our Lord in Victoria, British Columbia, 1875." Unpublished Undergraduate History Thesis, University of Victoria, 1964.

Edwards, Gail Elizabeth. "Creating Textual Communities: Anglican and Methodist Missionaries and Print Culture in British Columbia, 1858–1914." PhD diss., University of British Columbia, 2001.

Gould, Jan. *Women of British Columbia*. Saanichton, B.C.: Hancock House, 1975.

Helmcken, John Sebastian. *The Reminiscences of John Sebastian Helmcken*. Edited by Dorothy B. Smith. Vancouver: UBC Press, in co-operation with the Provincial Archives of British Columbia, 1975.

"Hills, George." ABCBookWorld [website]. http://www.abcbookworld.com/view_author.php?id=4995 (accessed June 4, 2010).

Hills, George. *No Better Land: The 1860 Diaries of the Anglican Colonial Bishop George Hills*. Edited by Roberta L. Bagshaw. Victoria: Sono Nis Press, 1996.

———. A Tour in British Columbia. London: Clay Printers, 1861.

Killian, Crawford. *Go Do Some Great Thing: The Black Pioneers of British Columbia*. Vancouver: Douglas & McIntyre, 1978.

Kirk-Montgomery, Allison, and Shelley McKellar. *Medicine and Technology in Canada, 1900–1950*. Transformation Series 16. Ottawa: Canada Science and Technology Museum, 2008.

Kluckner, Michael. Victoria the Way it Was. North Vancouver, B.C.: Whitecap Books, 1986.

O'Keefe, Betty, and Ian Macdonald. *Disaster on Mount Slesse: The Story of Western Canada's Worst Air Crash*. Madeira Park, B.C.: Caitlin Press, 2006.

Ormsby, Margaret A. *British Columbia: A History*, Vancouver: Macmillan Company of Canada, 1958.

———. "Douglas, Sir James." *Dictionary of Canadian Biography Online*. Vol. 10, *1871–1880*. University of Toronto/Université Laval, 2000. http://www.biographi.ca/009004-119.01-e.php?&id_nbr=4955&interval=20&&PHPSESSID=uiggt850s17c17orv46ukap3g4 (accessed April 10, 2010).

———. "Douglas, Sir James." The Canadian Encyclopedia, n.d. http://www.thecanadianencyclopedia.com/index.cfm?PgNm=TCE&Params=A1ARTA0002373 (accessed April 10, 2010).

Peake, Frank A. *The Anglican Church in British Columbia*. Vancouver: Mitchell Press, 1959.

Pethick, Derek. *Men of British Columbia*. Saanichton, B.C.: Hancock House, 1975.

Pollit, Sean, Anne Wicks, Cassandra Morton, and Caroline Duncan. Philanthropists, Child Saviours and the Founding of the British Columbia Orphans' Home [website]. "Edward and Mary Cridge." Victoria: University of Victoria, History Department, n.d. http://web.uvic.ca/vv/student/orphans/founders.html (accessed April 10, 2010).

Reformed Episcopal Church (Anglican). Diocese of Western Canada & Alaska and the Mission District of Cuba [website]. "The History and Founding Principles of the Reformed Episcopal Church." Victoria, B.C., 2009. http://www.recwcan.ca/pivot/history.php (accessed May 17, 2010).

Reformed Episcopal Church of Canada. Diocese of Ontario [website]. http://www.rececan.org/ (accessed May 17, 2010).

Roberts, Charles G. D., and Arthur L. Tunnell, eds. *A Standard Dictionary of Canadian Biography: The Canadian Who Was Who*. Vol. 2, *1875–1937*. Toronto: Trans-Canada Press, 1934–38.

Story, Vernon, et. al. *The Home: Orphans' Home to Family Center, 1873–1998*. Victoria: Cridge Center for the Family, 1999.

Walbran, John T. *British Columbia Coast Names, 1592–1906*. Ottawa: Government Print Bureau, 1909.

Watters, Reginald Eyre, ed. *British Columbia: A Centennial Anthology*. Toronto: Mc-Clelland & Stewart, 1958.

Woodcock, George. *Amor De Cosmos: Journalist and Reformer*. Toronto: Oxford University Press, 1975.

ABOUT THE AUTHORS

IAN MACDONALD was born and educated in Glasgow and worked for several years on Scottish newspapers before moving to Canada. He was a reporter in Ontario and Alberta before finding his way to the West Coast where he worked on the *Victoria Colonist*, the *Vancouver Province* and the *Vancouver Sun*. He was Ottawa correspondent for the *Sun* for five years before becoming press officer for Prime Minister Pierre Elliot Trudeau. He later took a job with the Ministry of Transport where he produced an award-winning documentary film prior to becoming an author.

BETTY O'KEEFE was born in Vancouver and began writing for the *Province* newspaper while attending Magee High School. She took a full time job there after two years at the University of B.C. where she worked on the student newspaper, the *Ubyssey*. She resigned her *Province* job after seven years to have a family but returned to the work force in 1967. She quickly moved into the field of public relations as a consultant and later as supervisor of communications for a large canadian corporation. In 1988, she opened her own company O'Keefe Communications, but decided to move on to writing books in 1994. Since then, O'Keefe and co-author Ian Macdonald have written ten books.

Index

Poll, Abigail Irene, 159–60
Presbyterian Church, 100, 133, 152–53, 162
Princess Royal (ship), 41, 55
Raby, John, 14–15, 42, 122
Raby, Mrs. John, 14–15, 42, 122
racism, 25, 33, 45, 49–50, 61–64, 66, 82, 87, 103, 108–9
Reece, Archdeacon William, 127–28, 130–131
Reformed Episcopal Church, 135, 140–41, 147, 170–71
Roman Catholic Church, 32, 53, 76–77, 87–89, 91–92, 100, 130
Ross, Charles, 27
Royal Charlie (ship), 82
Royal Navy base, 26, 39, 65, 82, 94, 137, 155
Rupert's Land, 25
Scott, Rev. M., 96
Sellindge Cottage, 112–13
Service, Robert, 150, 159
sexism, 55, 81, 95–97, 100, 105, 116
sexual mores, 19, 61, 96–97
Seymour, Frederick, 117, 119
"silent Sundays," 99, 152–55
Simpson, George, 25
smallpox epidemic, 94–95
Society for the Propagation of the Gospel, 78, 132

Songhees, **48**, 48–51, **50**, 61, 81
St. Ann's school, 56, 88
St. John's Church (Langley), 71
St. John's Church (Victoria), 79, 126, 139
St. Paul's Church (Esquimalt), 137
St. Paul's Church (Nanaimo), 39–40
Staines, Emma, 32–33
Staines, Rev. Robert, 8–9, 11, 32–34
Taylor, John George, 122–23
Teague, John, 142
telegraph line, 73, 116–17
Tierra del Fuego, 20
Tynemouth (ship), 95–97, 144
union of the colonies of Vancouver Island and British Columbia, 45, 73, 83, 101, 117–18
Victoria Directory, 97, 100
Victoria Gazette, 61
Victoria school, 40, 54–56
Waddington, Alfred, 57, 108–9
Wells Fargo, 61, 94
Wesleyan Methodist Church, 50–51, 87, 89–91, 100
West Ham, 5, 7–8, 169
wilderness, 8–9, 27, 39, 70, 79, 86
Winmill, Mrs. George, 12–14
Wood, Rev. Charles, 107
Wright, Archdeacon Henry P., 158
YMCA, 52–53, 117

Marquis imprimeur inc.

Québec, Canada
2010